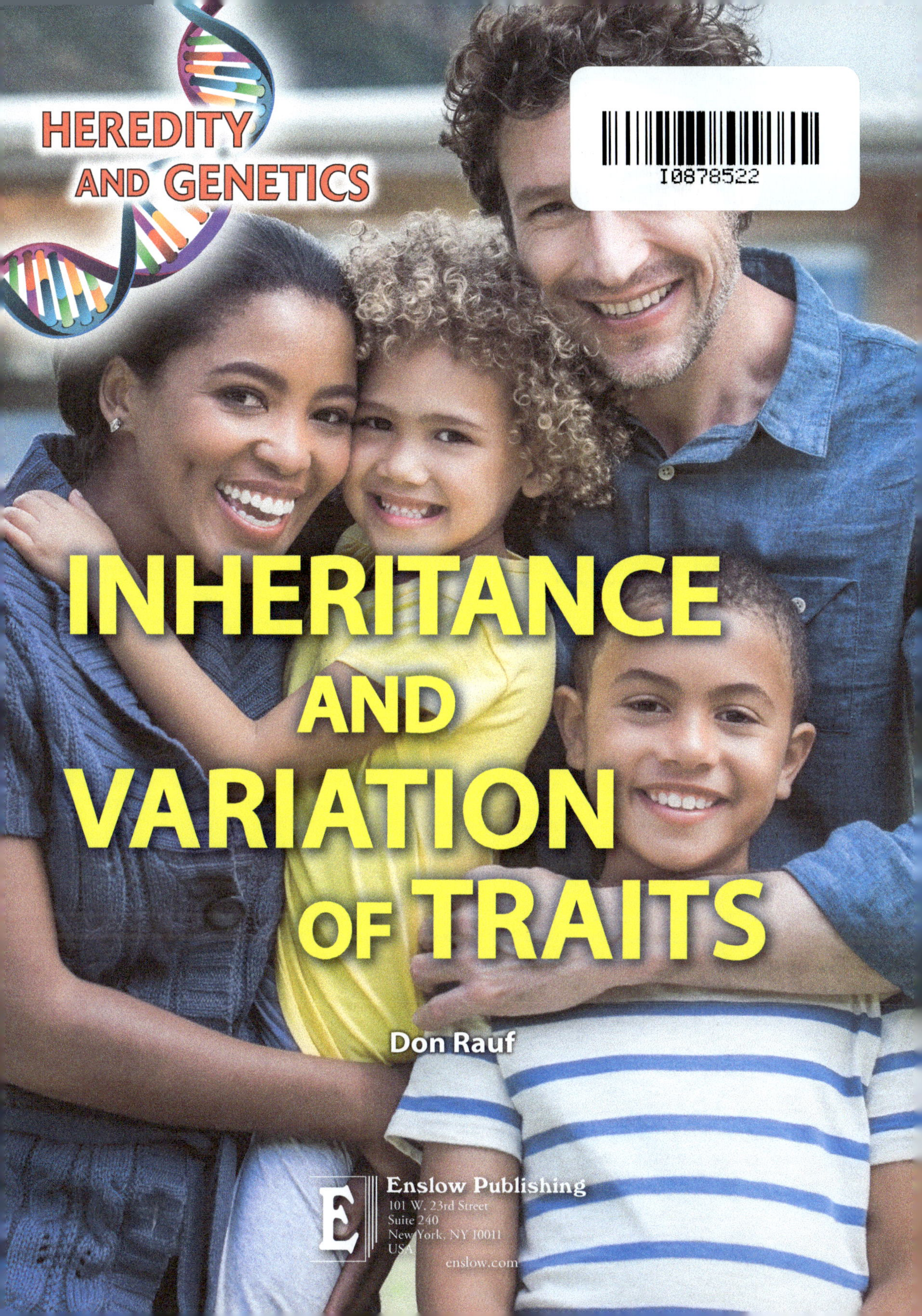

HEREDITY AND GENETICS

INHERITANCE AND VARIATION OF TRAITS

Don Rauf

Enslow Publishing
101 W. 23rd Street
Suite 240
New York, NY 10011
USA
enslow.com

Published in 2019 by Enslow Publishing, LLC
101 W. 23rd Street, Suite 240, New York, NY 10011

Library of Congress Cataloging-in-Publication Data

Names: Rauf, Don, author.
Title: Inheritance and variation of traits / Don Rauf.
Description: New York, NY : Enslow Publishing, LLC, 2019. | Series: Heredity and genetics | Audience: Grades 7-12. | Includes bibliographical references and index. | Identifiers: LCCN 2017051703| ISBN 9780766099357 (library bound) | ISBN 9780766099371 (paperback)
Subjects: LCSH: Genetics—Juvenile literature. | Heredity—Juvenile literature.
Classification: LCC QH437.5 .R39 2019 | DDC 576.5—dc23
LC record available at https://lccn.loc.gov/2017051703

Printed in the United States of America

To Our Readers: We have done our best to make sure all websites in this book were active and appropriate when we went to press. However, the author and the publisher have no control over and assume no liability for the material available on those websites or on any websites they may link to. Any comments or suggestions can be sent by email to customerservice@enslow.com.

Portions of this book originally appeared in *Introduction to Genetics* by Carol Hand.

Photo credits: Cover, p. 1 Portra Images/DigitalVision/Getty Images; p. 4 Blend Images/Shutterstock.com; p. 8 DEA/G. Dagli Orti/De Agostini/Getty Images; p. 10 Spencer Arnold/Hulton Archive/Getty Images; p. 14 Bettmann/Getty Images; pp. 18, 24, 41, 48 Designua/Shutterstock.com; p. 20 joshya/Shutterstock.com; p. 22 Spencer Sutton/Science Source; p. 27 Laguna Design/Science Source; p. 29 Martin Shields/Science Source; p. 33 wassei/Shutterstock.com; p. 35 Sam Wirzba/Passage/Getty Images; p. 37 Sia Kambou/AFP/Getty Images; p. 40 NLM/Science Source/Getty Images; p. 43 Alila Medical Media/Shutterstock.com; p. 46 Martin Fowler/Shutterstock.com; p. 52 Biophoto Associates/Science Source/Getty Images; p. 55 Capreola/Shutterstock.com; p. 57 Zvitaliy/Shutterstock.com; p. 59 Universal Images Group North America LLC/Alamy Stock Photo; p. 63 Pallava Bagla/Corbis Historical/Getty Images; p. 66 David Parker/Science Photo Library/Getty Images; p. 68 Pascal Goetgheluck/Science Source; interior page headers Juli Hansen/Shutterstock.com (DNA strand); interior page backgrounds and back cover paulista/Shutterstock.com (DNA double helix).

Contents

Children usually resemble their parents because they inherit physical characteristics through their genes.

Introduction

You may have heard the phrase: "like father, like son," or "like mother, like daughter." The reason we may be like our parents is all due to heredity and genetics. Genes are made up of DNA, or deoxyribonucleic acid. Genes are often called the blueprint of life because they tell cells what to do and when to do it. All the functions of all the cells in your body, including their life and death, are regulated by genes.

Genetic coding tells our body cells how many times they can divide and keep us living on. In theory, the human body could never live much longer than a maximum of one hundred twenty years because our genetic coding sets a limit on how many times our cells can divide. In 2013 *NBC News* reported that Carmelo Flores Laura (1890–2014) of Bolivia was the oldest living human documented at 123 years old.

Why does someone live so long? Many scientists would say it's partially because of good genes that they inherited from their parents. Heredity is the passing of genes from one generation to the next. A person's physical attributes—such as brown eyes, baldness, height, and skin color—are all inherited from parents. (Plants and animals pass along qualities as well.) Personality traits and characteristics get passed along, too. So if you're smart, creative, and musical, for instance, you may have your parents to thank.

And your parents got their traits from their parents and so on and so on. If you take the theory to it's extreme, we all got our traits from the earliest humans on Earth. In fact, a group of geneticists in 1987 concluded that all people on Earth could trace their lineage back two hundred thousand years to a single female ancestor who they dubbed Mitochondrial Eve. (Mitochondria are the power generators in every cell.)

So why aren't we all exactly alike since we all descended from the same earliest humans? Believe it or not, in many ways we are all the same—scientists estimate that all human beings are 99 to 99.9 percent identical in their genetic makeup. It's that tiny remaining fraction that makes all the difference.

Even though all human DNA makeup is so close, there can be more than three million differences between your genome and someone else's. The genome is the complete set of genes or genetic material present in you or any other organism. The genome variations exist because of mistakes or mutations that have been made along the way as DNA sequences have been reproduced.

Today scientists have a better idea of how genes, DNA, and heredity work. By manipulating genes through genetic engineering, researchers have developed ways to design plants that can resist harsh conditions, make drugs that are more effective and safer, and potentially prevent or cure deadly diseases. The hope is that the more we understand about genetics, the more we can improve our lives and the world we live in.

1

The Genesis of Genetics

The practice of cultivating plants and herding animals—basically what we call farming—dates back ten thousand to twelve thousand years ago to the Fertile Crescent. This Middle Eastern region stretched from the Persian Gulf, through modern-day southern Iraq, Syria, Lebanon, Jordan, Israel, and northern Egypt. The farmers here understood that if they chose to breed animals and plants with useful characteristics, those characteristics could show up in the offspring. Seeds from the fullest grains often produced heartier grains. Cows and goats that were strong milk producers had offspring that were equally abundant. Although the farmers did not understand how genetics worked, they had a basic grasp on the concept that traits could be inherited.

Although babies from strong healthy animals usually had the desired traits, they didn't always. Early farmers did not understand why sometimes traits showed up in the next generation and sometimes they didn't. It would be a long road of scientific discovery to completely understand how genetics and inheritance worked.

Although they did not understand genetics, ancient Egyptian farmers understood that favorable traits in animals and plants could be passed on to their offspring.

The Early History of Genetics

In 400 BCE, the Greek philosopher Hippocrates (c. 460–c. 370 BCE) suggested that seeds or particles produced in the bodies of both parents were blended. He thought this explained why a child showed characteristics of both parents. Aristotle (c. 384–322 BCE), another Greek philosopher, did not agree. He said it could not be true because some children do not resemble their parents.

For more than two thousand years, people mostly accepted the idea of "blending inheritance."

Darwin and the Theory of Evolution

During the nineteenth century, science changed forever. Instead of guessing, two men separately collected and analyzed large amounts of data. They developed theories to explain what they saw. One of these men was Charles Darwin (1809–1882), who developed the theory of evolution. The other was Gregor Mendel (1822–1884), now known as the "father of genetics."

From 1831 to 1836, Charles Darwin worked as the naturalist aboard the British ship HMS *Beagle*. During this voyage, Darwin collected plants, animals, and fossils at every stop. He recorded detailed observations of their structures and habitats. He noticed that organisms varied by habitat. For example, South American plants and animals looked different from the same types in Europe. Most people then believed living creatures and plant life on Earth had never changed. Darwin began to question this belief. His observations led him to think life constantly changed, or evolved. His examinations of living things showed they were adapted to their environments. His observations of fossils suggested new species could evolve over very long time periods.

Darwin continued to observe nature for many years after he returned to England. He figured out patterns in his data and tried to explain them. Finally, in 1859, he published a book, *On the Origin of Species*, which described his theory of evolution. Although another naturalist named Alfred Russel Wallace (1823–1913) independently developed the same concept, the theory bears Darwin's name because he published his observations before Wallace and he did a great deal more research.

Charles Darwin believed that organisms evolved, inheriting traits that helped them adapt to their environment and increase their chances of survival.

How Natural Selection Drives Change

Darwin's theory of evolution deals with changes within populations. A population is a group of organisms of the same species that live in the same place. Evolution describes changes to populations over long periods of time. The changes are very tiny, but they occur over many generations. Darwin's theory proposes a process by which these changes occur.

A theory is a well-tested explanation of how something happens. It describes a process by which all the facts came to be. Darwin's theory describes how populations adapt, or change as their environment changes, through a process called natural selection. Darwin defined natural selection as the "principle by which each slight variation [of a trait], if useful, is preserved." Natural selection relies on two factors. One factor is the presence of inherited variations, or differences, which all organisms have. These variations are obvious in family members. Family members look similar, so you can tell they are related. But they are not identical. The differences are inherited variations. The other factor is stress caused by the environment. Environmental stress might be lack of food or presence of competing species or predators. It might also be a change in climate.

According to Darwin, all species undergo a "struggle for existence." For example, what if some plants in a population withstand hot, dry conditions better than others? In hot, dry years, these plants still reproduce and leave many new plants to form the next generation. Plants that die more quickly in hot, dry weather leave fewer offspring. The next generation has more plants that can survive hot, dry conditions. If the weather stays hot and dry for many years, the "hot, dry" trait builds up. Plants that don't have it decrease in number. If most years are mild, both traits will be present in more equal numbers.

Darwin's theory began to explain heredity. His observations described changes in traits through generations and convinced him that natural selection occurred in populations. But he could not explain how traits were transferred between individual organisms. Future scientists would figure out the mechanism for passing change from generation to generation.

Darwin tried to explain it by "pangenesis," or "whole birth." He suggested body cells shed tiny pieces called "gemmules," which collected in reproductive organs and helped determine the offspring's characteristics. But Darwin had no evidence for pangenesis. How natural selection happened remained a puzzle.

One missing piece of Darwin's puzzle was published in 1866, only seven years after his own work. This paper, called "Experiments in Plant Hybridization," was by an Augustinian friar named Gregor Mendel. Mendel gave evidence and proposed a method for passing information about traits from parent to child.

The Monk Who Became the Father of Genetics

The future "father of genetics" was born on July 22, 1822, in Heinzendorf, a village that is now part of the Czech Republic. In 1843 Johann Mendel entered the Abbey of St. Thomas in Brünn. He took the name Gregor. The Abbey had scientific instruments, a large botanical collection, and a library of more than thirty thousand books. It also had extensive gardens. The friars were teachers, university professors, and researchers. They encouraged Mendel's interest in science. In 1851 the Abbot (head of the monastery) sent Mendel to the University of Vienna. There, he studied physics and botany. Physics taught him to use

DARWIN VS. MENDEL: BLENDING VS. NONBLENDING

Charles Darwin and Gregor Mendel both made significant contributions to how we understand inheritance of traits. Through his observations, Darwin determined that organisms and populations change over time. They take on traits from their parents that will help them with survival and reproduction. Over time, each new generation becomes increasingly well-prepared for their environments. Darwin called the process "descent with modification": we call it evolution. Organisms evolved according to natural selection, which has also been described as "survival of the fittest." Basically, organisms produce more offspring than can survive. The ones that do survive pass on the traits that have made them more likely to survive.

Darwin believed that traits were passed down through blending. For example, if a tall person reproduced with a short person the result would be a medium-sized person. Mendel discovered that the mechanism of heredity is nonblending. Genes do not blend. Traits are wholly inherited, but some are dominant and some are recessive. A trait that is dominant will be seen more frequently in each generation. A recessive trait might disappear in one generation but then reappear in a following generation.

Gregor Mendel discovered the basic laws of inheritance through his work on pea plants.

experiments and mathematics. Botany stimulated his interest in plant variation and inheritance.

When he returned to the monastery, Mendel spent most of his time in the gardens. From 1856 to 1865, he conducted studies of inheritance in garden peas. Unfortunately, Mendel's one published paper was ignored during his lifetime. It was not rediscovered until 1900, sixteen years after his death.

Progress from Pea Plants

Mendel needed a test species to show inheritance patterns. He chose garden peas because they had many traits that were present in two—and only two—forms. These "either-or" traits were easy to distinguish. Seeds were either yellow or green. Plant stems were either long or short. Flowers were either purple or white. Mendel studied seven pairs of these simple traits: seed shape (smooth or wrinkled), flower color, seed coat tint, pod shape (constricted or inflated), unripe pod color (green or yellow), flower location (at the side or the end of the stem), and plant height.

Peas can self-fertilize because the flowers contain both male and female parts. New plants form when a plant's pollen fertilizes its own egg cells. Mendel studied only pea plants that "bred true." That is, ones that, when self-fertilized, produced offspring that always looked exactly like the parents. This meant Mendel could be sure of the ancestry of each plant.

Mendel also chose peas because he could pollinate them by hand. First, he removed the stamens from a flower before it produced pollen. This prevented the plant from self-pollinating. Then he used a small paintbrush to dust mature pollen from another plant onto the flower. This cross-pollination produced hybrid plants.

For eight years, Mendel grew and tested between twenty-eight thousand and thirty thousand pea plants. He made sure all pea varieties were true-breeding by counting the offspring from every cross. Then he began cross-pollinating plants with specific traits. First, he tested one trait at a time. Later, he tested combinations of two and three traits. By carefully counting the offspring of thousands of crosses, Mendel collected a wealth of data.

2 The Fundamentals of Inheritance

When Gregor Mendel crossed two pea plants to develop a hybrid variety, he crossed purebred plants, offspring of many generations that has the same form of the trait as its parents. With his garden peas, Mendel tested "either or" traits. For example, a pea was either tall or short; wrinkled or smooth. He collected huge amounts of data and mathematically analyzed the results from thousands of crosses. From his exhaustive research and testing of his hypothesis, he yielded three laws of inheritance: the law of dominance, the law of segregation, and the law of independent assortment. Mendel's crosses and his thought processes are complicated. They must be followed step-by-step.

When One Trait Is Crossed

First, Mendel reasoned that peas inherited two "factors," one from each parent, which determined a trait. He tested this hypothesis by doing monohybrid crosses. For example, he crossed a plant that bred true for yellow seeds with one that bred true for green seeds. These two plants were the mother and father in his cross.

MENDELIAN INHERITANCE

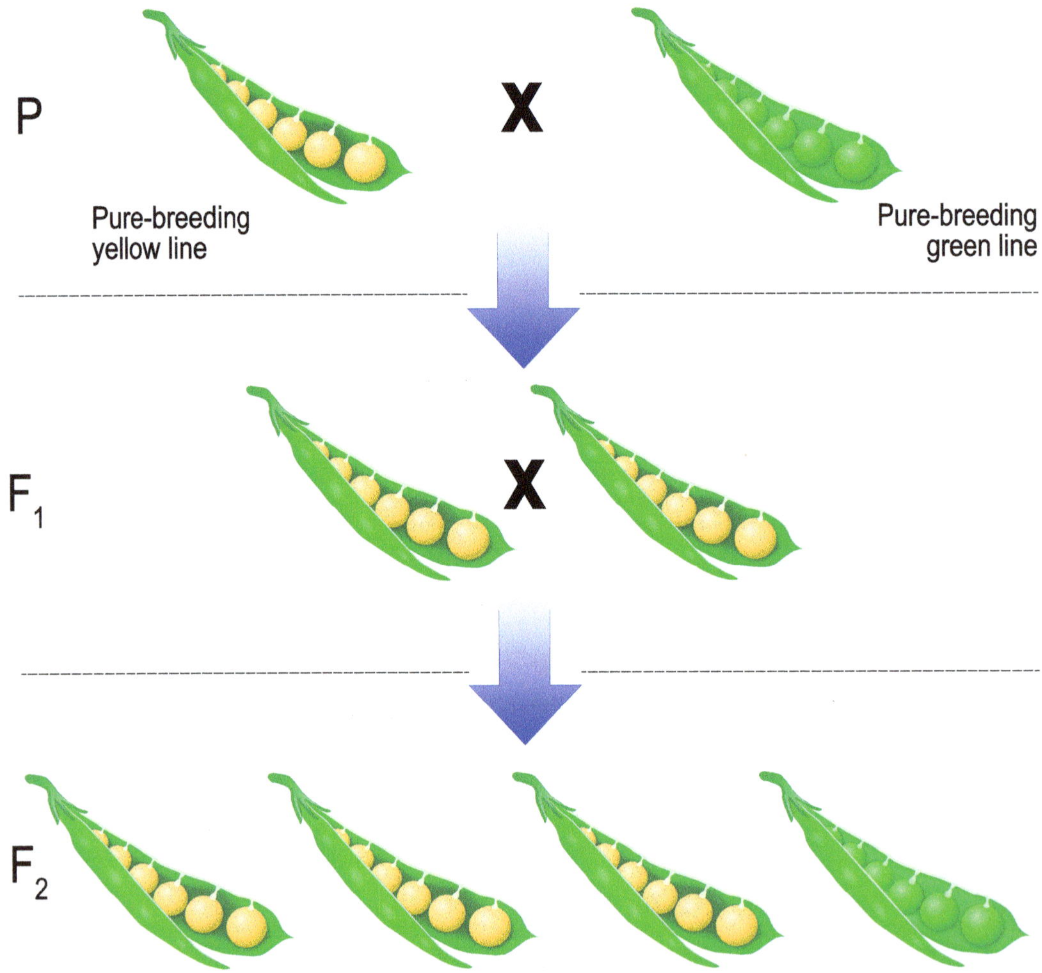

Mendel found that a dominant trait (here, yellow seeds) could mask a recessive trait. The recessive green trait showed up in the third generation.

They were the first (parent) generation. This cross produced a second generation with all yellow seeds. The yellow-seed trait is dominant because it completely masks the presence of the green-seed trait. The masked form (green seeds) is recessive.

But the recessive trait did not disappear. Mendel proved it still existed by allowing members of the second generation to self-fertilize. This produced a third generation in which one-fourth of the seeds were green.

Discovering a Dominant Factor

What Mendel called "factors" causing pea traits, are now called genes. The two forms of each gene—the "either-or" factors, such as yellow or green seeds—are called alleles of the gene. An individual inherits two different alleles from each of its two parents. According to Mendel's law of dominance, the observable characteristics (phenotype) of only one allele are visible in the offspring, making it the dominant allele.

Mendel's Breakthrough

The third generation had both pure yellow and pure green seeds. There were no blended forms. That is, crosses of yellow and green seeds did not produce yellowish-green or greenish-yellow seeds. The same held true for all traits tested. The fact that traits from both parents showed up unchanged in the third generation supported Mendel's hypothesis. This hypothesis became known as the "theory of particulate inheritance," which says that traits are determined by factors (genes) that pass unchanged from generation to generation. This conclusion was a breakthrough in the study of inheritance. It disproved the old idea of "blending inheritance."

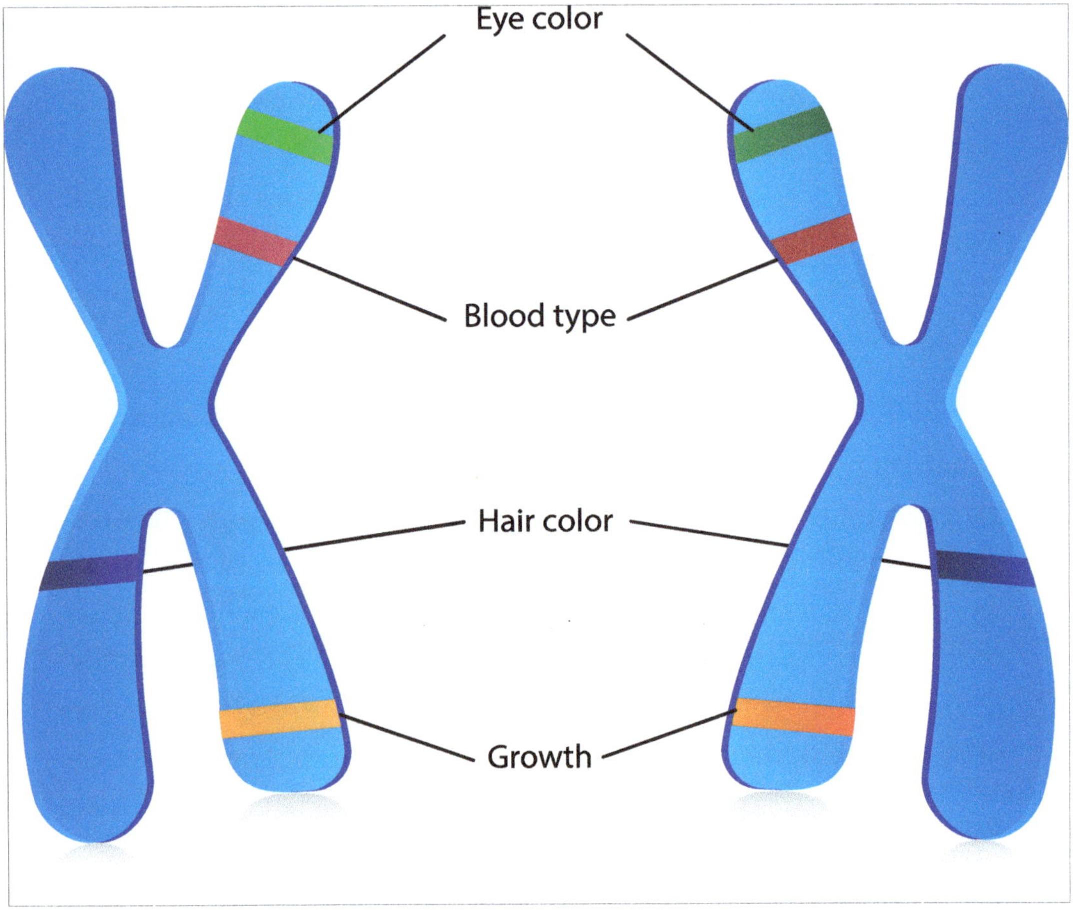

Alleles are copies of a gene that differ from each other. They are responsible for variations in traits such as eye color, hair color, and blood type.

During Mendel's time, people knew nothing about cell structures that determined inheritance. Still, Mendel deduced what happened inside the cell. He reasoned that the two separate factors sorted randomly in each parent and entered the sex cells. In peas, the egg and pollen grain would each contribute one factor to determine a trait such as seed color. If each second-generation parent produced equal numbers of each type of sex cell (for example, "green-seed" and "yellow-seed" cells), there was an equal chance of the offspring receiving either type. From these data, Mendel deduced the law of segregation. This law states that pairs of factors (alleles) segregate (or separate) randomly and unchanged into separate sex cells (gametes).

Your mother and father will each have two genes for hair color. You, the offspring, get one gene from each but it is random which one. Related to this is Mendel's law of independent assortment, which basically determined what the allele—a sex cell—gets from one gene does not affect what allele comes from another gene.

REDISCOVERING MENDEL'S WORK

For decades, Mendel's theories about heredity went unnoticed in the scientific community. Mendel's mathematical models were unfamiliar at the time. According to strictly observational methods, many biologists believed in the concept of blending when it came to inheritance. In 1900 the scientists Hugo de Vries (1848–1935), Carl Correns (1864–1933), and Erich von Tschermak-Syenegg (1871–1962) rediscovered Mendel's laws. Although they were all working independently on studies regarding plant hybrids, cells, and chromosomes, they all came to the same conclusion that Mendel was right.

The law of independent assortment states that separate traits are passed independently of one another on to offspring. Here, in the third generation, nine out of sixteen plants had smooth, yellow seeds; three out of sixteen had wrinkled, yellow seeds; three out of sixteen had smooth, green seeds; and one out of sixteen had wrinkled, green seeds. Alleles for yellow and smooth seeds are dominant over the green and wrinkled seeds.

Genes for independently assorted traits are located on different chromosomes or separated on the same chromosome.

Learning the Lingo of Genetics

Mendel crossed visible traits (phenotypes) and counted the different phenotypes that appeared in the offspring. From his data, he deduced the combination of alleles producing each phenotype, which is called the genotype. The genotype is hidden inside the cell's DNA.

Scientists use a shorthand way to describe alleles in genotypes. A capital letter stands for the dominant allele. For example, *Y* stands for yellow seeds. The lowercase *y* stands for the recessive allele of the same gene, such as green seeds. Each parent gives one allele—*Y* or *y*—to each offspring. So, offspring have one allele from each parent to make a pair for each trait.

Some genotypes have two alleles of the same type. If both alleles are either dominant (*YY*) or recessive (*yy*), they are called homozygous genotypes. Other genotypes, *Yy*, have one recessive and one dominant allele. These are called heterozygous genotypes.

A Square to Picture Combinations

Reginald C. Punnett (1875–1967), an English geneticist, developed the Punnett square. This diagram can predict outcomes of crosses. It illustrates the results of a cross by showing all possible genotype combinations. It shows how recessive traits persist in a population. It also shows how different alleles segregate during sex cell formation and regroup in offspring.

This Punnett square shows a monohybrid cross:

		Alleles in sperm	
		Y	**y**
Alleles in eggs	**Y**	**YY**	**Yy**
	y	**Yy**	**yy**

PUNNETT SQUARE

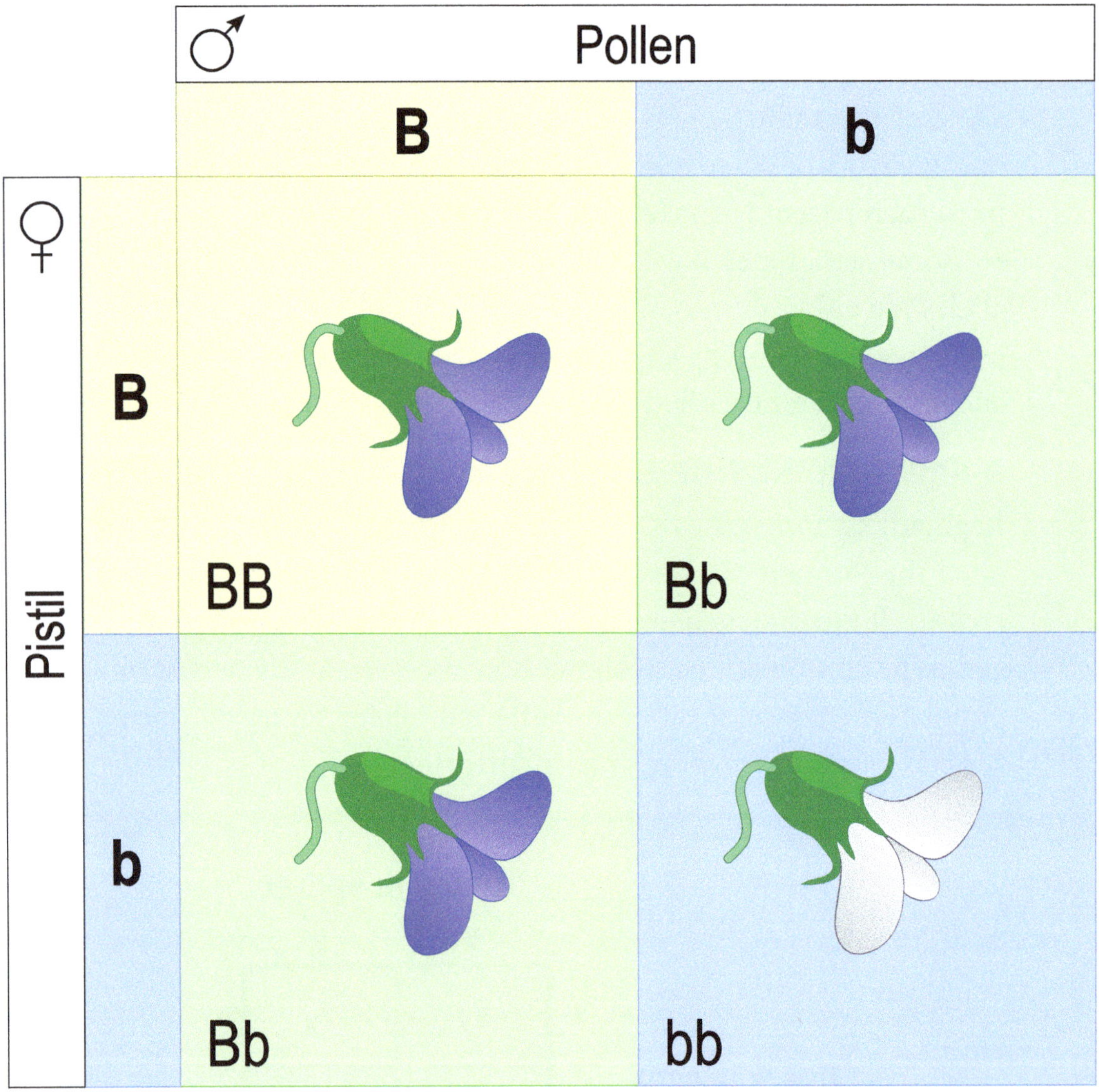

This Punnett square diagrams a typical cross of pea plants and potential outcomes of homozygous dominant (*top left*), heterozygous dominant (*top right and bottom left*), and homozygous recessive (*bottom right*) genotypes.

The *Y* and *y* alleles across the top are the yellow and green alleles—the sperm—in the pollen grain from a heterozygous plant can donate. The *Y* and *y* alleles on the left side are possible alleles from the egg. The four squares inside the box show how the heterozygous parents' alleles can pair at fertilization. These pairs represent the only four possible combinations of two alleles.

A monohybrid cross of two heterozygous parents can produce three possible genotypes in the next generation:

• A *YY* offspring receives a dominant allele from each parent and has a yellow phenotype. All of this plant's sex cells will have the dominant *Y* allele.

• A *Yy* offspring has one dominant and one recessive allele. Yellow is dominant over green, so the green allele is masked, and *Yy* genotypes also have yellow phenotypes. It makes no difference that the dominant *Y* allele came from the mother in one *Yy* offspring and from the father in the other. Half of the sex cells produced by these plants will contain the *Y* allele. The other half will have the *y* allele.

• The *yy* has two recessive alleles. No dominant alleles are present to mask the recessive allele, so these offspring all appear green. This genotype is the "1" in Mendel's 3:1 ratio.

The three offspring with the dominant trait—*YY, Yy,* and *Yy*— represent the "3" in Mendel's 3:1 ratio. No matter how many plants he crossed, three out of every four offspring showed the dominant phenotype.

3

Predicting the Odds

Probability is a mathematical way of measuring the likelihood of something happening. To get a good measure of probability, scientists often rely on the law of large numbers. In an experiment that is repeated a large number of times, the frequency of the outcome tends to be what the probable outcome will be in the future. By analyzing a large number of plants and results, Mendel developed his theories. When Mendel cross-fertilized pure purple plants with pure white plants, all the resulting plants were purple. Then when he let the new purple offspring plants self-pollinate, he found that about three out of four plants were purple and one was white in this new second generation of plant. He successfully used probability theory to estimate the frequency with which characteristics would be passed on.

Mendel knew the parents in his earliest crosses were true-breeding. But he did not know the offspring's genotypes. He did testcrosses to determine this. A testcross is a cross between an individual and its homozygous recessive parent type. For example, Mendel might cross a yellow offspring (*Yy*) from the second generation with its green (*yy*) parent type.

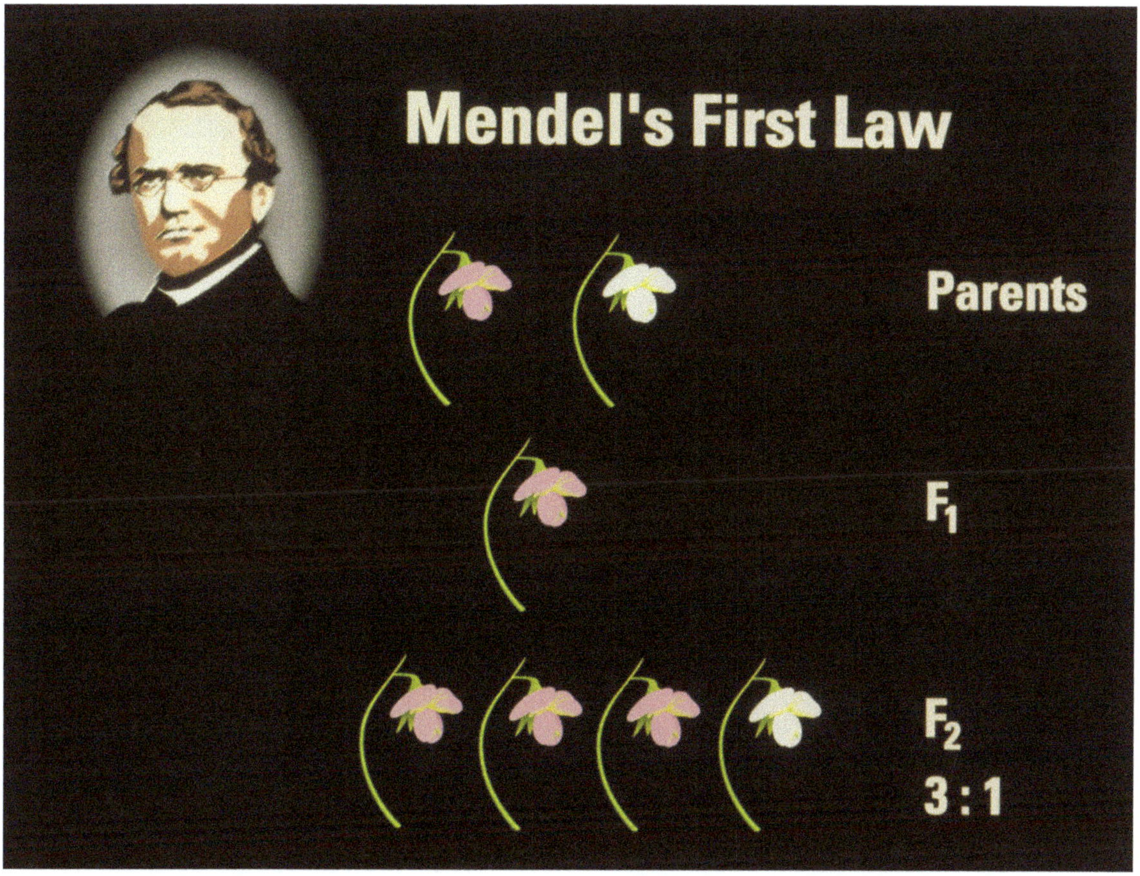

The law of segregation, also known as Mendel's first law of genetics, shows how purple and white parents produce a first generation of purple flowers. Self-pollinating gives a 3:1 ratio of purple to white flowers.

The offspring of such a testcross might have either a *Yy* or a *yy* genotype. Punnett squares can predict the results of crossing an individual with each genotype with one that is homozygous recessive. If the genotype of the individual is homozygous dominant (*YY*), as shown in the left square on the next page, all offspring will have yellow phenotypes. If the genotype of the individual is heterozygous, or *Yy* (right square), half will be yellow and half will be green. By comparing the actual results of the cross with the predictions shown in the Punnett square, a researcher can determine the individual's genotype.

Mendel's testcrosses of second generation offspring backcrossed with their green parent gave the needed information. These results showed the genotype of the second generation was heterozygous, not homozygous, because the green trait appeared. It also showed there were equal numbers of green and yellow alleles. If alleles had not sorted randomly (and equally), the seeds would not have been half yellow and half green.

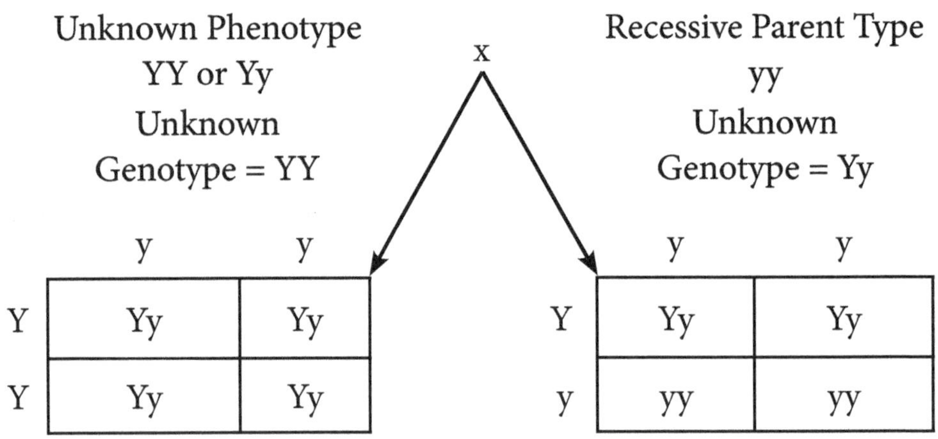

Mendel also thought "factors" for different traits were not connected to each other. He thought genes controlling different traits were independent and traveled separately when they entered gametes. To test this hypothesis, he conducted dihybrid crosses, using combinations of two genes.

The following Punnett square shows a dihybrid cross using two different pairs of alleles—round (*R*, dominant) and wrinkled (*r*, recessive) seeds, and tall (*T*, dominant) and short (*t*, recessive) plants. Each parent donates one allele from each of the two pairs. So, the possible gametes, shown outside the square, have two

By experimenting with garden pea traits, Mendel discovered that a wrinkled seed shape is recessive while a smooth texture is dominant.

alleles, not one, and the offspring inside each box have two pairs of alleles.

		Alleles in Sperm			
		TR	Tr	tR	tr
Alleles in Eggs	TR	TTRR	TTRr	TtRR	TtRr
	Tr	TTRr	TTrr	TtRr	Ttrr
	tR	TtRR	TtRr	ttRR	ttRr
	tr	TtRr	Ttrr	ttRr	ttrr

A dihybrid cross has sixteen possible combinations of two gene pairs. As always, whenever a dominant allele is present, that allele appears in the phenotype. In the top row above, all four genotypes have at least one dominant allele for both height and seed shape. So, all four will have tall, round phenotypes. In the second row, all four have at least one tall allele, but two have the *rr* genotype, which will be wrinkled. So, of these four, two will be "tall, round" and two will be "tall, wrinkled." Combining all similar phenotypes in this way gives a set of predictable mathematical ratios:

9/16 tall, round
3/16 tall, wrinkled
3/16 short, round
1/16 short, wrinkled

In shorthand form, this is a 9:3:3:1 ratio. Remember that a monohybrid cross has three different genotypes. For seed color, these are *YY*, *Yy*, and *yy*. A dihybrid cross has nine different possible genotypes. For plant height and seed shape, these were:

TTRR	TTRr	TTrr
TtRR	TtRr	Ttrr
ttRR	ttRr	ttrr

Mendel also did trihybrid crosses involving three traits. When he tested traits for height, seed shape, and seed color together, the same thing happened, only with more possible combinations. Three pairs of genes have twenty-seven possible genotypes.

In Mendel's dihybrid crosses, every possible combination of traits appeared in the offspring in these predictable ratios. Inheritance patterns for each trait were the same whether they were tested separately or together. This suggested that alleles for the different traits sorted and traveled randomly. They followed the laws of probability.

THE MENDEL CONTROVERSY

In the early twentieth century, the British statistician Ronald Fisher (1890–1962) suggested that Mendel's data matched too closely to the values he was expecting to get. Basically, Fisher initially thought that the data was too good to be true. He calculated that there was only about a .00007 chance that his data could match his theoretical probabilities. Ultimately, Fisher praised Mendel for his scientific work and viewed his experiments as demonstrating truths. Some have suggested that Mendel may not have fudged the numbers on purpose, but he may have collected data until the numbers were closely in agreement with his theories. While some scientists have now questioned how he may have crunched the numbers, many of his theories on heredity have been upheld by other research

This confirmed Mendel's hypothesis about the law of independent assortment. It states that, during formation of gametes, different pairs of genes sort randomly and travel separately into the egg or sperm cell.

Later geneticists found things are not always so simple. Gregor Mendel, however, set the stage for the development of the entire field of genetics. His laws of inheritance formed the basis for all research that followed.

4

Going Beyond Mendel's Laws

As scientists began to delve deeper into the study of inheritance, they started to find limitations in the patterns of inheritance that Mendel had identified. Mendel did not know there would be exceptions to some of his laws. Researchers discovered that not all traits are completely dominant or recessive, and some traits do appear to blend. Many traits are controlled by more than one gene at different locations on the chromosome.

Blending Is Sometimes Possible

In Mendel's peas, self-crossing heterozygous purple flowers produced a 3:1 ratio of purple to white flowers in the next generation. That is, purple was completely dominant over white. But some other crosses produce a different result. When a pink snapdragon is self-crossed, half the flowers are pink. One-fourth of the offspring are homozygous (*RR*) and red, one-half are heterozygous (*Rr*) and pink, and the other one-fourth are homozygous recessive (*rr*) and white.

This situation is called incomplete dominance. One allele for a specific trait is not completely expressed over its paired allele. Both red and white alleles show some dominance, but neither completely masks the presence of the other.

Pink snapdragons can demonstrate incomplete dominance. During self-crossing, neither the red or white allele is completely dominant, and half the flowers are pink.

Equal Expression of Traits

In codominance, two or more alleles are both expressed when present in only one "dose." Expression of the alleles is both independent and equal. One example is the inheritance of roan fur color in cattle. They have alleles for red and white coat color, named C^R and C^W. C stands for coat color. The capital letters R and W indicate that both colors are dominant. When a red bull (C^RC^R) is crossed with a white cow (C^WC^W), the resulting offspring have the genotype C^RC^W). They are all roan-colored. That is, they have a mixture of red and white hairs. The colors are equally expressed or codominant. The hairs are not pink, as in incomplete dominance. The animals have approximately equal numbers of red and white hairs, so they look mottled or speckled.

More Than Two Alleles

The system of ABO blood types in humans illustrates both codominance and another complex inheritance pattern—multiple alleles. Multiple alleles can make it possible for many dominance relationships. The human species has three different alleles that determine ABO blood types. Of course, each individual receives only two of these—one from each parent. Two of the three alleles, called I^A and I^B, are codominant. The third allele, *i*, is recessive. The dominant alleles cause the production of proteins, either Antigen A or Antigen B, on the surfaces of red blood cells. The recessive allele does not produce an antigen.

Three possible alleles combined in pairs gives six possible genotypes. They can produce four different phenotypes—blood groups A, B, AB, and O. The table shows the combinations of genotypes and the phenotypes they produce.

Blood Type (phenotype)	Possible Genotype
A	I^AI^A or I^Ai
B	I^BI^B or I^Bi
AB	I^AI^B
O	ii

People with Type A or Type B blood can be homozygous for the dominant allele. They can also be heterozygous, having

Codominance is when two different alleles of a specific single-gene trait are both expressed simultaneously. An example is in the red and white color hairs of roan cattle.

one dominant and one recessive allele. People with Type AB blood always have two codominant alleles. People with Type O blood always have two recessive alleles.

One Characteristic, Two or More Genes

Many traits in a population show continuous variation. That is, there is a range of variation, but no precise groups, such as red

HOW THE ENVIRONMENT AFFECTS GENE EXPRESSION

Changes in genes from one generation to the next don't just come from within. Sometimes the environment can influence gene expression. A dramatic example was demonstrated by the researcher C. R. Stockard in 1907. He placed fertilized fish eggs in seawater mixed with a chemical called magnesium chloride. The chemical in the seawater produced "cyclops" fish that had a single eye instead of the normal pair of eyes. Drugs and chemicals in the environment can have a profound effect on the genetic development of future generations. Temperature and sunlight can also affect the genetic makeup of an organism. Over time, the Himalayan rabbit has acquired genes that change the color of its fur. At lower temperatures, the fur becomes darker to retain heat and help it stay warmer.

versus white color. Human traits such as hair, eye, and skin color are good examples. These continuous traits result from polygenic inheritance. They are controlled by two or more gene pairs instead of one.

Hair, eye, and skin color result from melanin, a dark pigment. Two genes (A and B) control melanin production for skin color. Melanin production is dominant. Lack of production is recessive.

Albinism is a congenital disorder characterized by partial or complete lack of pigment in the skin, hair, and eyes. It is caused by recessive alleles.

A person who is homozygous recessive for both genes (*aabb*) produces no pigment. That person has albinism, a condition where he or she has very light skin, hair, and eyes. A person with only one dominant allele (*Aabb* or *aaBb*) is very light-skinned. A person with two dominant alleles (*AAbb, AaBb,* or *aaBB*) has medium skin color. A person with three dominant alleles (*AABb* or *AaBB*) has very dark skin, and one with all dominant alleles (*AABB*) has completely black skin.

A similar situation exists for hair and eye color. Melanin colors the iris of the eye. The more melanin produced, the darker the eye color. One main gene controls eye color. Dominant allele *B* controls production of brown, green, hazel, or gray eyes. Recessive allele *b* controls production of blue eyes. A blue-eyed person has very little melanin. But several other genes control the amount and distribution of melanin, so there is a continuous range of eye colors, as there is a continuous range of skin colors.

5

Cell Reproduction: Passing on Genetic Information

Mendel's laws of inheritance all come into play during the process of meiosis. Meiosis is a type of cell division required for sexual reproduction. The process reduces the number of chromosomes in the parent cell by half. The end result is four gametes, each with half as many chromosomes as the original cell. This process is required to produce egg and sperm cells. Other cells in humans and most animals, however, divide via a process called mitosis. During mitosis, a cell divides once to form two identical cells. Mitosis is how our body's grow and replace worn out cells. Skin, heart, stomach, hair cells, etc. all depend on mitosis.

Chromosomes Are Key

Walther Flemming (1843–1905), a German anatomist, used a microscope to investigate cell nuclei and find out more about nature of genetic information or how it was transferred. Flemming stained the cells with dyes. This produced a very dark network of fibers inside the nucleus. Flemming named it "chromatin." He saw that during nuclear division (mitosis), the network became a series of threadlike bodies. These structures were eventually named chromosomes.

The Details Are in the DNA

Mitosis transfers genetic information from cell to cell. It begins with the DNA molecule. Most of the DNA in higher organisms resides in the cell nucleus. The DNA of each chromosome is divided into genes. Each gene controls or helps control a single trait. Together, all the genes control all the traits that make up the body's structures and functions.

Each organism has a specific number of chromosomes. Humans have forty-six chromosomes in twenty-three pairs. Mendel's garden peas have fourteen chromosomes in seven pairs. This is the diploid, or $2n$ number, of chromosomes.

If a cell is going to divide, it grows to a certain size. Then, it duplicates its DNA. The two DNA copies separate and the cell divides to form two new cells. Each new cell now has one complete copy of the DNA. So, the two new cells, called "daughter cells," are identical to the

Walther Flemming performed early research on chromosomes. He was able to visualize the threadlike material as the cells divide.

original (mother) cell. This sequence may be repeated, becoming a cell cycle.

Step-by-Step Through Mitosis

The cell spends up to 90 percent of its time in interphase, before mitosis begins. During interphase, the cell increases in size and its DNA replicates.

When the cell contains two copies of all of its DNA, it's ready for mitosis. The first stage is prophase. DNA molecules shorten

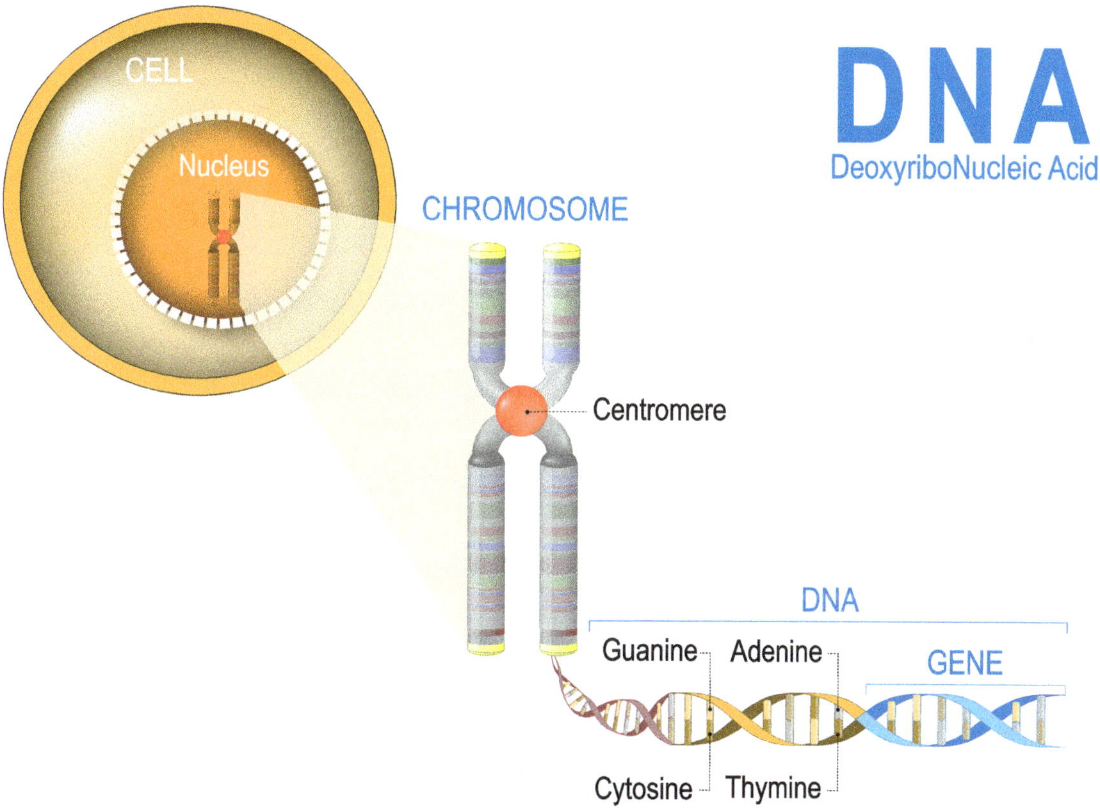

In the nucleus of each cell, the DNA molecule fits into chromosomes, which carry genetic information in the form of genes.

and coil into compact, visible chromosomes. They are spread randomly through the cell. They are double structures with two parts, or chromatids, held together by a centromere. Each chromatid contains one copy of the DNA. During prophase, the nuclear membrane begins to disappear and two structures called centrosomes migrate to opposite sides of the cell.

Then comes metaphase. The centromeres of all the chromosomes line up in single file down the center, or equator region of

CANCER: MITOSIS GONE WRONG

Cancer is a genetic disease caused by changes to genes that lead to uncontrollable division of abnormal cells in the body. They spread, invade nearby tissues, and stop healthy organs from doing their jobs. Cancer cells are able to ignore signals that normally tell cells to stop dividing. A change in DNA triggers the oncgene to turn on and this leads to wild cell reproduction via mitosis. Alterations in tumor suppressor genes and DNA repair genes can also lead to mutations that cause cancer. Doctors try to eliminate or control cancer with drugs, surgery, radiation, and other treatments. More recently, scientists have developed gene-altering treatments for cancer. In October 2017, the Food and Drug Administration approved a new class of treatment that genetically transforms patient cells so the immune system will kill cancer.

Mitosis

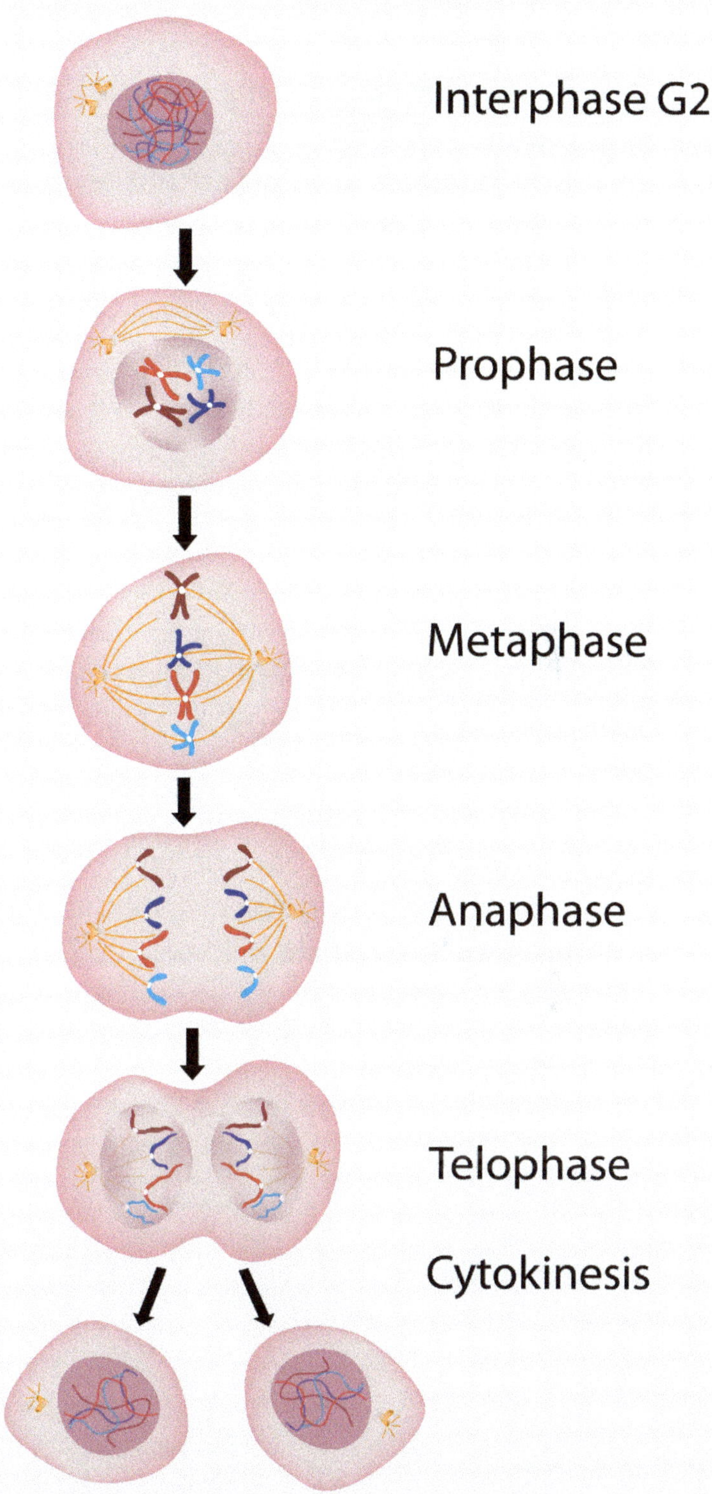

During mitosis, there are five stages leading up to cytokinesis, when the cytoplasm of a single cell divides into two daughter cells.

the cell. The chromatids hang over each side of the center line. Each chromosome moves independently, so they can line up in any order. Members of a pair are not necessarily near each other in line. Spindle fibers stretch between each centromere and the two centrioles, which are located at opposite poles of the cell.

During anaphase, centromeres break apart and separate the chromatids. They travel to opposite sides of the cell. As soon as they separate, the chromatids are now called chromosomes. In animal cells, a spindle fiber from the centriole attaches to each centromere and pulls it away from the middle of the cell. In telophase, the two sets of DNA have completely separated from each other. A new nuclear membrane forms around each set. The chromosomes relax and return to their interphase state. Near the end of telophase, the entire cell divides. A new cell membrane forms around each set of DNA. This cell-separation process is called cytokinesis.

As a result of mitosis and cytokinesis, one cell becomes two. Each new cell has one complete copy of the body's DNA, containing all the genes. The cell still has the diploid number of chromosomes: forty-six in humans.

6

Reproduction Leads to Genetic Variation

When gametes from two different parents come together to form a new individual, different gene combinations occur and that leads to genetic variation. A change in a DNA sequence called mutation adds to variation. Evolutionary change is due to the accumulation of many mutations. A mutation can cause a favorable genetic variation that helps an organism survive. This trait can then be passed down from one generation to the next. For example, some plants have developed flowers through genetic variation that resemble insects. This attracts insects and helps pollinate the plants. Gene flow, or migration, can also be a contributing factor to variation. This occurs when organisms or the genetic material they carry travel from one population to another. For example, pollen can blow from one area to a new destination and that will create new variations of plant life.

The Early Study of Meiosis

At the turn of the twentieth century, American Walter Sutton (1877–1916) studied meiosis in the lubber grasshopper. He identified its eleven pairs of chromosomes, plus a single sex chromosome. He described the stages of meiosis, following the

The bee orchid evolved to have flowers that look like bees to attract pollinating bees, which transfer pollen when they land on the flower.

progress of each chromosome. Most importantly, he argued that Mendel's "factors" moved into sex cells by meiosis. Sutton's 1902 paper was the first statement of the "chromosomal theory of inheritance."

Then, in 1903, Sutton made another major breakthrough. He knew half the chromosomes had come from the grasshopper's father and half from its mother. But they did not line up on "mother" and "father" sides during gamete formation. Instead, chromosome pairs lined up randomly down the cell center before dividing. When they separated into new cells, different gametes received different combinations of parental traits. Thus, Walter Sutton was the first person to explain how formation of sex cells results in variation.

Various Causes of Genetic Variation

Sutton showed that sexual reproduction causes variation, which requires a different type of cell division—meiosis. Gametes produced during meiosis have only half as many chromosomes as cells produced during mitosis. That is, they have only half as much genetic information. Also, genes are often rearranged during meiosis. These gametes have slightly different gene combinations than the person who made them.

Variation also occurs during fertilization, when an egg and a sperm cell fuse to form a zygote. Each parent has slightly different alleles. So, fertilization gives the offspring a new mixture of alleles—half from the mother and half from the father. The offspring has some characteristics of both parents but is identical to neither.

Cell Division: Round 1

Meiosis occurs in two parts. The key difference from mitosis occurs during Meiosis I. This is when reduction division occurs and the chromosome number decreases by half. A gamete begins as a regular body cell in the ovary or testis. It has the diploid number of chromosomes. During interphase, this cell duplicates its DNA and makes doubled chromosomes, with two chromatids each—just like mitosis.

In prophase of Meiosis I (Prophase I), the nuclear membrane disappears. The DNA shortens and coils to form visible chromosomes, as in mitosis. The chromosomes are randomly

MEIOSIS

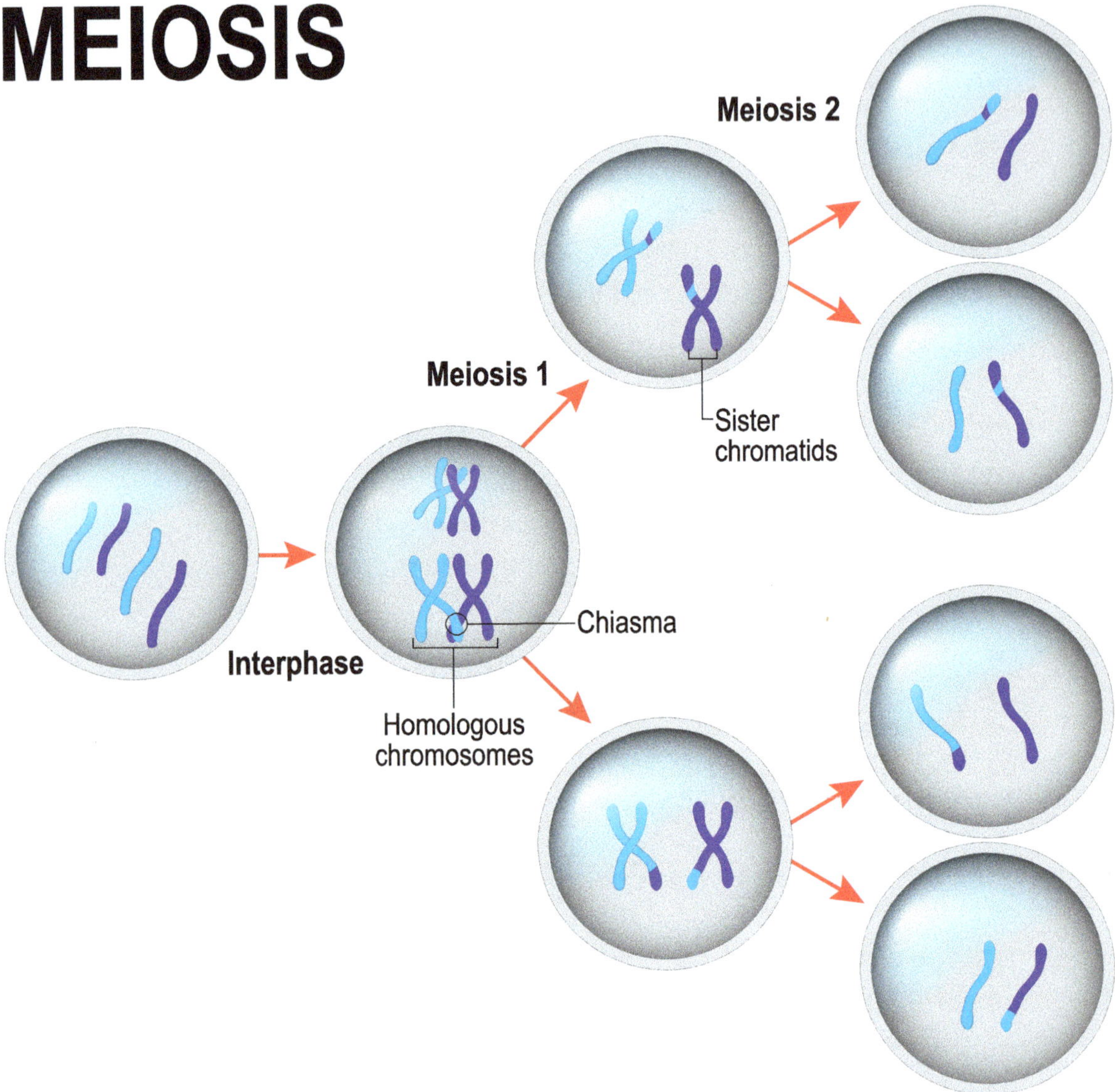

Gametes are generated through meiosis. Each resulting cell is haploid, containing one-half the number of chromosomes as the original cell.

mixed, and the centrioles begin to migrate to opposite poles of the cell.

But Metaphase I is different from mitosis. During meiosis, the chromosomes do not line up in single file down the center of the cell. Instead of forty-six individuals, they become twenty-three pairs. Members of homologous pairs find each other and line up side by side, one on either side of the cell's centerline. Spindle fibers stretch from each centromere to the centrioles of the two poles.

Often, when homologous chromosomes pair during metaphase, a special process called "crossing-over" occurs. Two of the four chromatids "tangle" and end up exchanging pieces. This changes the arrangement of alleles on the homologous chromosomes. Some of the original mother's genes are now on the original father's chromosome, and vice versa. When the chromosomes separate, each gamete has a new combination of alleles. Crossing-over is one way meiosis creates variation in gametes.

During anaphase of Meiosis I, the paired chromosomes—some now with different gene combinations—move apart and go toward opposite sides of the cell. This is the second way variation occurs during meiosis. Homologous pairs have separated forever.

In Telophase I, nuclear membranes form around the two new sets of chromosomes. Chromosomes return to their relaxed interphase state. Cytokinesis occurs. At the end of Meiosis I, there are two new cells. Each cell has a reduced chromosome number—half the number in the original cell. This is the haploid, or *n*, number. Each gamete will give only half the parent's genes to an offspring.

Cell Division: Round 2

Both new cells now carry out a second division, Meiosis II. This time, the nuclear material divides by exactly the same process as mitosis. Each new cell gets one chromosome (consisting of a single chromatid with one copy of the DNA) for each homologous pair in the original cell. Meiosis II begins with two cells, so the end result is four cells. Because of reduction division and crossing-over in Meiosis I, all are different from the original starting cell.

Gametogenesis, or gamete formation, is not complete when chromosomes separate. In human males, cytokinesis during Meiosis II results in equal division of the cytoplasm. It ends with four cells of the same size. These four cells begin to change shape. Most of the cytoplasm forms into a long tail. Gametogenesis in males makes four tiny but functional sperm cells. All of the father's genetic material is preserved. Not all of it will be used because only one sperm can fertilize an egg. Nevertheless, it is all available.

In females, nuclear division happens exactly the same as in males. But the division of cytoplasm is unequal. One daughter cell in Meiosis I receives most of the cytoplasm, so it is bigger than the other. The same thing happens during Meiosis II. The largest cell becomes an egg cell. The other three cells, called polar bodies, die. So, any mother cell forms only one functional egg cell. One-half the mother's genetic information is lost.

Fertilization: Completing the Genetic Mix

Genes are thoroughly mixed during meiosis. Crossing-over occurs in Metaphase I. Paired chromosomes separate randomly in Anaphase I. Genetic information is lost when an egg is formed. So the eggs and sperm produced are considerably different

A GENETIC MUTATION LED TO MILK DRINKING

Although some people are lactose-intolerant, most people today can drink milk and eat dairy products such as cheese. According to an article in *Nature* in 2013, that wasn't always the case. A study from Institute of Archaeology at Mainz University in Germany found that about seven thousand years ago, the large majority of European adults could not tolerate milk at all. It was basically like a poison to them because the adults could not produce the lactase enzyme required to break down lactose, the main sugar in milk. As farming increasingly replaced hunting and gathering, humans evolved. They reduced lactose by fermenting milk and creating cheese. Then humans developed a genetic mutation that spread through Europe and allowed adults to produce the gut enzyme needed to break down the lactose.

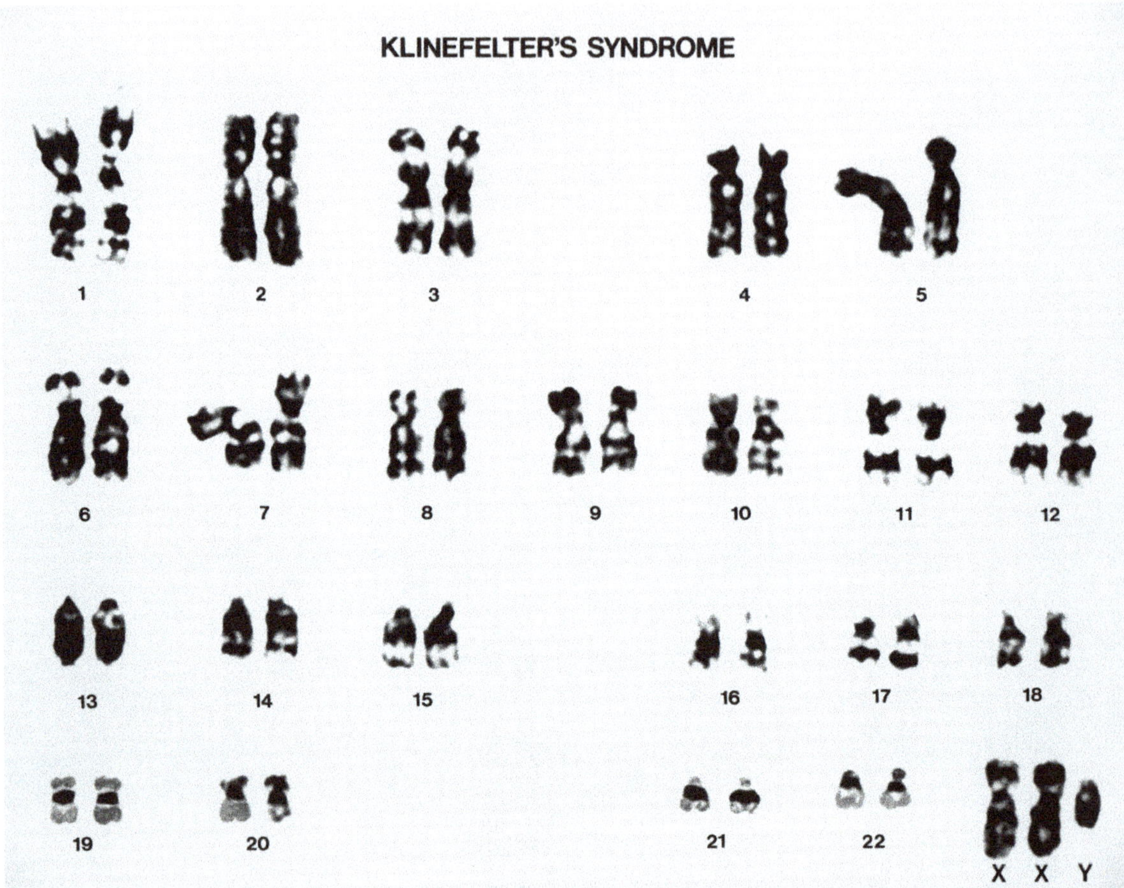

Klinefelter syndrome is a chromosomal condition that affects male development. Most often, it results from the presence of one extra copy of the X chromosome in each cell.

from the parent's starting cell. Meiosis and gametogenesis have produced variation.

Fertilization causes more variation. Because of reduction division, human egg and sperm cells have only twenty-three chromosomes each—one member of each pair, randomly selected from the original pair. From millions of sperm cells produced, only one will fertilize the egg cell. The genetic mix of this one lucky sperm cell will be entirely random. In humans only one egg cell per month will mature and be available for fertilization. When the single set of genes in the egg combines with the single set in the sperm, the third and final form of variation occurs. The mother's and father's genes will mix and form an entirely new combination of genes. The result will be a unique individual.

Meiosis and Nondisjunction

Like mitosis, meiosis can sometimes go wrong. Sometimes, when chromosome pairs line up during Meiosis I, members of a chromosome pair stick together. Two chromosomes will go into the same cell and none will go into the other cell in that division. The resulting gametes will either have an extra chromosome or they will lack one. Failure of chromosomes to separate correctly during meiosis is called nondisjunction. It results in specific genetic disorders such as Down syndrome, Turner's syndrome, and Klinefelter's syndrome.

7

Linkage: Genetic Travel Companions

During the meiosis phase of sexual reproduction, certain DNA sequences that are close together on a chromosome will be inherited together. It is unlikely that genetically linked markers will separate into distinct chromatids. There is a lower chance of recombination, whereby pieces of DNA are broken and recombined to produce new combinations of alleles. Gene linkage has been one of the major exceptions to Mendel's law of independent assortment. Linkage decreases variation. In the pea plant, the position for the flower color and the pollen shape are on the same chromosome. Purple flowers and long pollen shape are dominant in pea plants. These traits are linked and inherited together.

How the Process Works

The simplest way to define linkage groups, or genes that travel together, is by the number of chromosome pairs in the cells of an organism. Humans have twenty-three pairs of chromosomes and twenty-three linkage groups. Mendel's peas have seven pairs

SEX CHROMOSOMES VS. AUTOSOMES

Out of the twenty-three pairs of chromomes you have, one pair is the sex chromosomes. The other twenty-two are all called autosomes. There are two types of sex chromosomes—X and Y. Females have two X chromosomes and males have an X and a Y. The Y chromosome is small compared to the X with 255 genes and 50 million base pairs compared to 1,141 genes and 150 million base pairs. The Y chromosome contains a gene, SRY, which triggers embryonic development as a male. Autosomes determine everything else except for sex. Physical characteristics, such as chin, earlobe, hairline, and thumb shape, are all inherited through the autosomes.

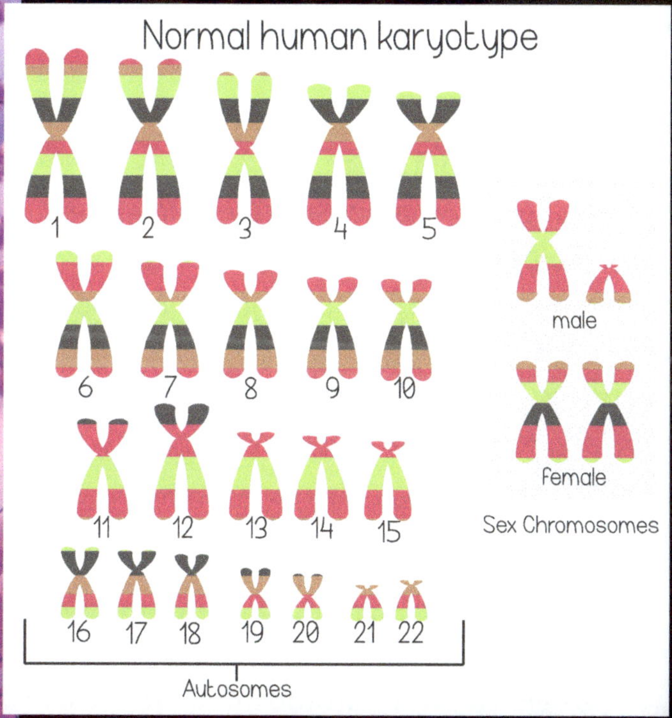

A karyotype is the number and appearance of chromosomes in the nucleus of a eukaryotic cell.

of chromosomes and seven linkage groups. But linkage is not this simple. Because of crossing-over, genes located on the same chromosome can still behave as though they are not linked.

To understand how linkage happens, it helps to understand something about the structure of DNA and chromosomes. A chromosome consists of a very long molecule of DNA associated with numerous protein molecules. This DNA molecule is made of tiny repeating units called nucleotides. Each nucleotide contains an even tinier unit called a base. There are only four types of bases in the DNA molecule: adenine (A), guanine (G), cytosine (C), and thymine (T). The DNA molecule consists of two strands, and the bases connect in specific pairs to hook the strands together.

The order, or sequence, of base pairs along the strand defines different genes. Genes vary greatly in length, but an average gene is about five thousand base pairs long. Each gene contains a code determined by the sequences of bases along its length. This genetic code tells the cell how to make a certain protein. Together, the body's proteins determine the structures, functions, and behaviors that make each person unique.

People have about 20,500 identified genes scattered along their chromosomes. Each gene helps make as many as six different proteins. Between the genes are long, repeating segments of non-coding (non-gene) DNA, often misleadingly called "junk DNA." Altogether, humans' forty-six chromosomes have almost three billion base pairs. Probably only about 5 percent of these are actually part of a gene.

The Likelihood of Linkage

The distance between any two genes is measured in numbers of base pairs. This distance determines how likely two genes are to be linked. In general, if two genes on a chromosome are closer

DNA Structure

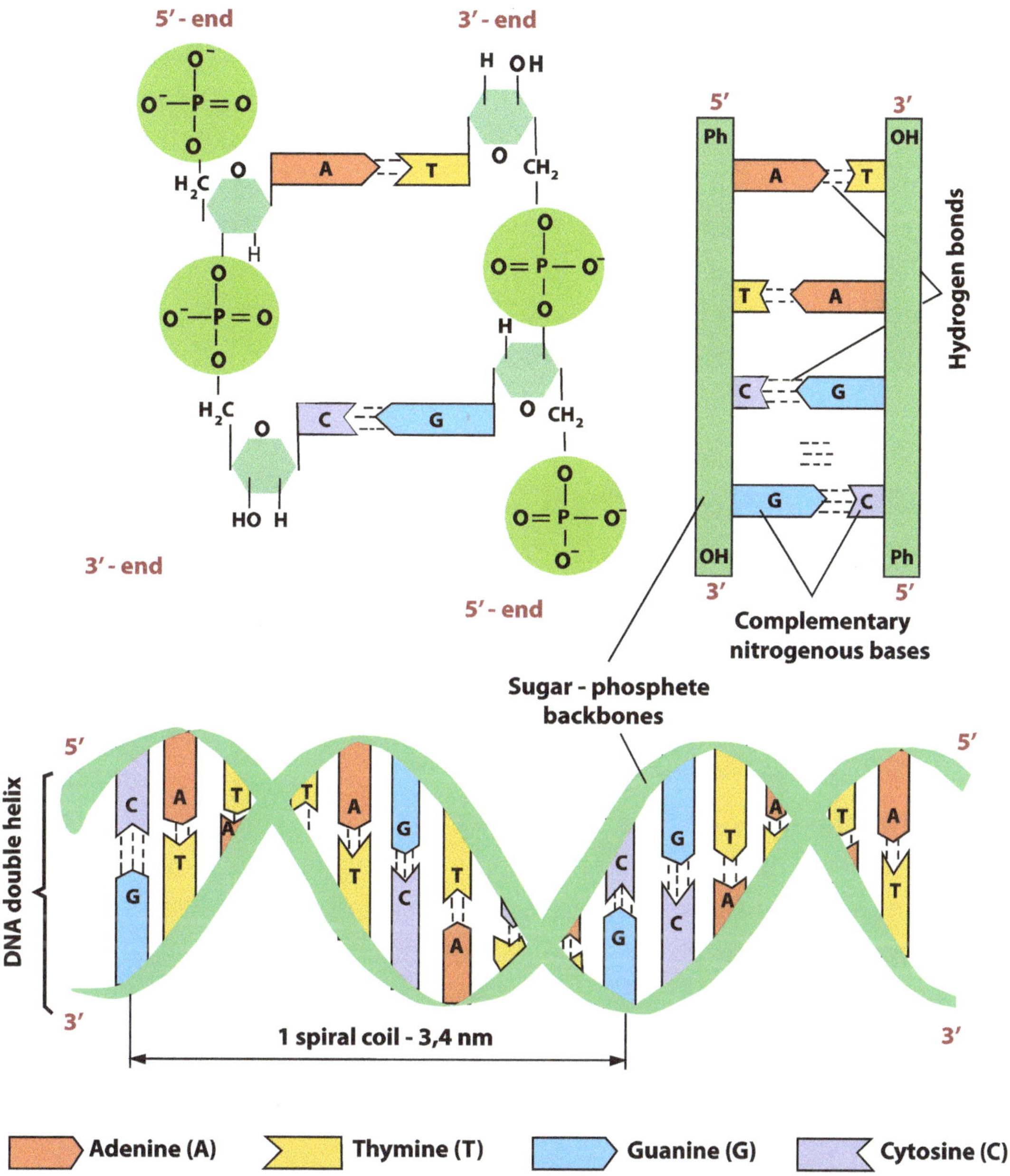

DNA is composed of nucleotides linked together by chemical bonds. A nucleotide is made up of one sugar molecule, one phosphate molecule, and one of the four bases.

than fifty million base pairs, they will be linked. That is, they are more than 50 percent likely to travel together when chromosomes separate during meiosis. They follow Mendel's law of independent assortment. But, if they are farther apart than fifty million base pairs, there is an increased chance they will *not* travel together. This is because of crossing-over.

The specific location of a gene along a chromosome is called its locus. If two gene loci are close together, crossing-over will probably not occur. But the farther apart the two loci are, the more likely it is that breaks and crossing-over will occur. If two genes are far enough apart, they act like they are on different chromosomes.

Fruit Flies and the Discovery of Linked Traits

American geneticist Thomas Hunt Morgan (1866–1945) won a Nobel Prize for discovering and describing patterns of gene linkage. Morgan and his students found that certain fruit flies have four pairs of chromosomes, including one pair of sex chromosomes. As in humans, females have two large X chromosomes and males have one much smaller Y chromosome. However, unlike the situation in humans, the fruit fly's Y chromosome does not determine its maleness—it is male if only one X chromosome is present and female if there are two. With only one X chromosome, there was never a dominant chromosome to mask the recessive allele.

Testcrosses with the white-eyed mutation led Morgan to question Mendel's laws. When he crossed red-eyed females with white-eyed males, first- and second-generation offspring both followed Mendel's laws. First-generation flies were all red-eyed and the second generation showed a 3:1 ratio of red to white. But, when he crossed white-eyed females with red-eyed males,

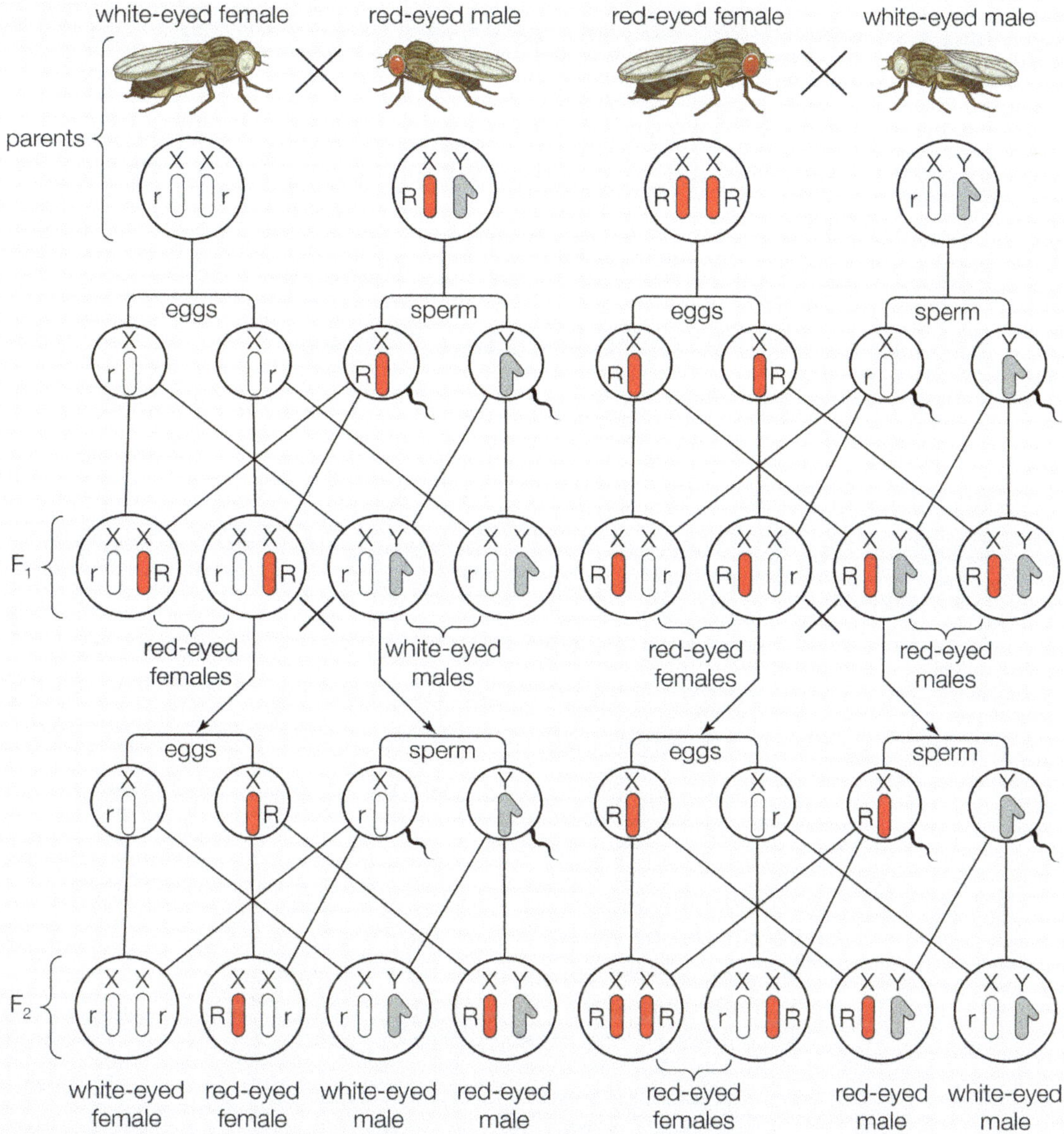

Experiments with red-eyed and white-eyed *Drosophila* flies helped scientists understand how traits were distributed in developing organisms and transmitted through successive generations.

both the first and second generations showed half red-eyed and half white-eyed flies. Morgan reasoned that this eye-color gene must be located on the X chromosome. The white-eyed allele was recessive, so it always showed up in males that possessed the allele because they have only one X chromosome (*rO*). The Y chromosome had nothing to do with it. The allele had an effect in females only when it was present as a double recessive (*rr*).

Getting Closer: When Genes Join Forces

A linkage analysis determines if genes on a chromosome are close enough to be considered linked. It shows how often crossing-over occurs between two or more genes. To do a linkage analysis, scientists do testcrosses between heterozygotes and recessive homozygotes and count the phenotypes of the offspring, just as Mendel did. If there is no linkage, all combinations of phenotypes will appear in approximately equal frequencies. If linkage is occurring, the proportions will be unequal. The table shows a 20 percent cross-over, with the two rarer phenotypes each being produced 10 percent of the time.

Linkage in a Dihybrid Testcross (AaBb x aabb)

Genotype	Proportion
Aabb	40%
aaBb	40%
AaBb	10%
Aabb	10%

The map distance is the amount of cross-over between genes at two loci. It is calculated by dividing the total number of recombinant (cross-over) offspring by the total number of offspring. The result, multiplied by one hundred, gives the percent of recombinants. In humans, one map unit on a chromosome represents about one million base pairs and one percent recombination.

8

Genetic Engineering: The Pursuit of a Better World

The mid-twentieth century was a great time of advancement in understanding genetics and DNA. In 1952 Rosalind Franklin (1920–1958), working with a student, was able to get high-resolution photos of crystallized DNA fibers. Based on Franklin's X-ray diffraction images, James Watson (1928–) and Francis Crick (1916–2004) created their famous two-strand, or double-helix, model showing the structure of DNA.

By 1966 Marshall Nirenberg (1927–2010), Har Khorana (1922–2011), Severo Ochoa (1905–1993), and their colleagues had cracked the genetic code. They figured out how genetic information inside a DNA molecule is organized in nucleotide sequences called genes. The genetic code is the relation between the sequence of bases in DNA and the sequence of amino acids in proteins.

These discoveries meant geneticists no longer had to study genes indirectly by looking at phenotypes. In 1972 they made the first recombinant DNA organism by splicing DNA from one species of bacteria into another species. Now, scientists could not only study actual genes, they could manipulate them. Genetic engineering had begun.

Manipulating Genes

Geneticists quickly realized the implications of DNA research. One was the promise of new and better foods and drugs. A gene

On the left, brinjals, a type of eggplant, have been attacked by fruit and shoot borer insects. On the right, the brinjals have been genetically modified to resist insect attack.

from another organism could now be spliced into a crop plant to make it more nutritious or disease-resistant. A cow can be engineered to produce more milk. Foreign genes are inserted into bacteria so they can produce drug products such as human insulin and human growth hormone.

Another promise of genetics is the ability to treat genetic disorders. This requires analyzing genomes. Understanding the genome of any organism requires long, painstaking work. It can be divided into two parts: gene sequencing and gene mapping.

A Call for Order: Base Sequences in DNA

A base sequence is the order of nucleotide bases in a sequence of DNA. This order determines the primary structure of the proteins encoded by the DNA. The four bases—adenine, thymine, cytosine, and guanine—can be abbreviated A, T, C, and G. A base sequence is a long list of these four letters with no spaces. They are not neatly divided into "words" or "sentences," so just looking at the sequence won't tell you what it means.

Base sequences are always huge. The bacterium *E. coli* contains a mere 4.6 million base pairs. Assuming three thousand characters per page, it would take 1,533 pages to print it all. Thomas Hunt Morgan's tiny fruit fly contains 180 million bases—that's sixty thousand pages. Most people would think the human genome has the most bases and genes. However, a grasshopper has 180 billion base pairs, and a single-celled amoeba has about 670 billion.

Many of the non-gene, or "junk," sequences in a genome are repeated over and over. Organisms with the largest genomes seem to have the most junk DNA. Until recently, people thought it had no function. But now they realize that some of it has a variety of cell functions, including regulating aspects of protein synthesis.

Deciphering the Human Genome

Scientists quickly began to work out base sequences of important research organisms. As they analyzed DNA, it became clear that many genes are almost identical in all organisms. Closely related organisms have more DNA in common. Half of fruit-fly DNA is identical to human DNA. Humans and mice have 85 percent of their DNA in common, and humans and chimpanzees have 98 percent. Not surprisingly, some identical genes act the same. Genes for smell or taste act the same in nematode worms as they do in humans.

Sequencing the human genome was the purpose of the Human Genome Project, first proposed in 1985. Scientists began the project in 1990, and in 2001, a "rough draft" of the human genome was published. A much improved and corrected version followed in 2004. The human genome still has gaps, but scientists in laboratories all over the world continue to work on this massive project.

Reading a Gene Map

Gene maps as well as base sequences are needed to understand genomes. A gene map is similar to a city map. It locates every gene precisely by placing it at the correct locus on the correct chromosome. One author compared locating a specific gene to locating a person in New York City given a picture but no name, address, or telephone number.

Like Alfred Sturtevant's first map of the fruit fly's X chromosome, gene maps are still basically straight lines with "markers," or locations of known genes or DNA sequences, identified along their lengths. Some are physical maps, showing the exact number of base pairs between markers. Others are gene-linkage maps, such as Sturtevant's. They show gene locations in

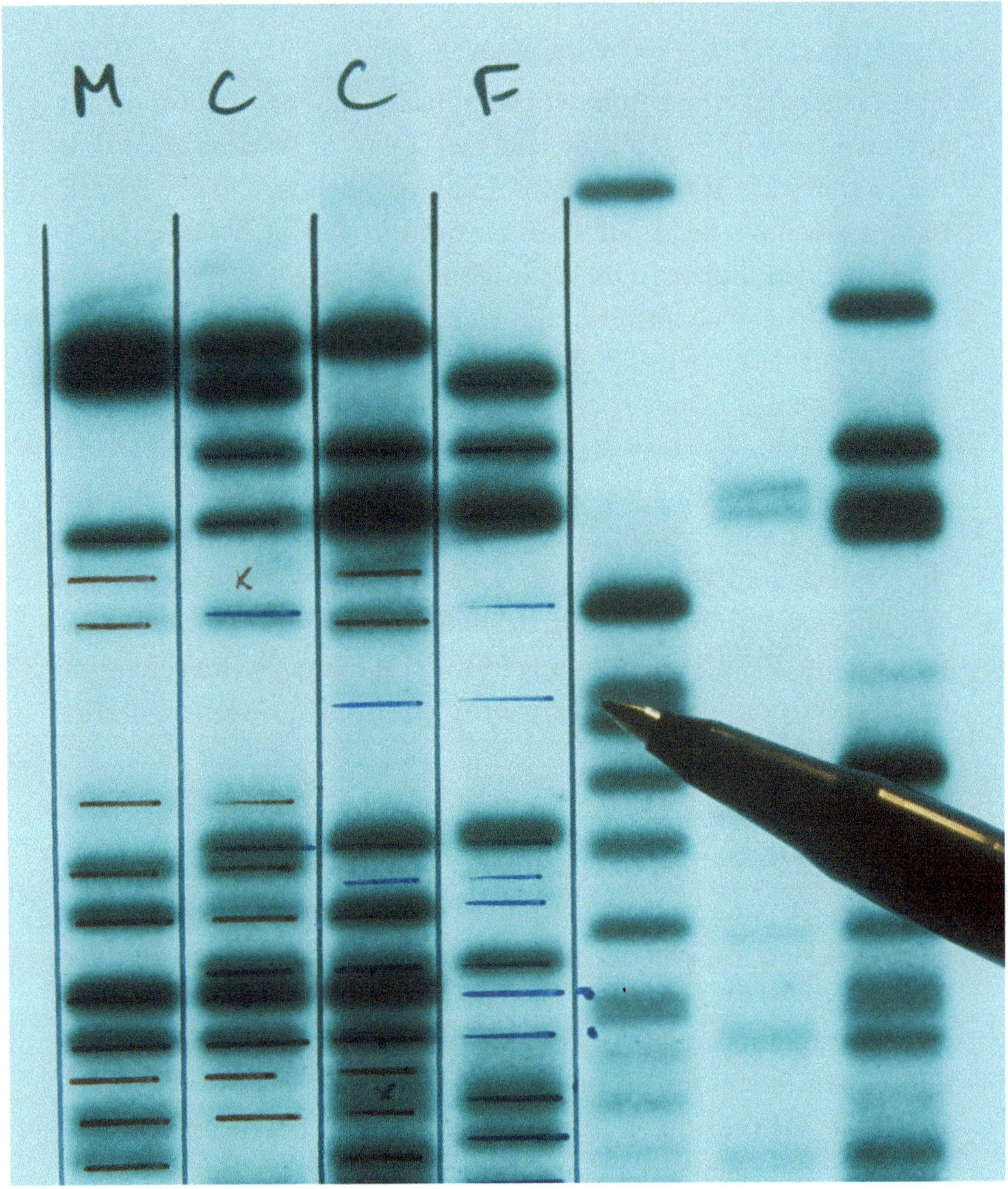

The pattern of DNA bands is unique to each individual, but some bands are shared by related people. The bands in these DNA fingerprints have M for mother (in red), C for child, and F for father (in blue). Both children share some bands with each parent, proving their relationship.

relation to each other, relative distances between genes, and likely linkage patterns. Sturtevant had only phenotypes to determine gene locations. Geneticists can now locate unique, non-repeating DNA sequences, which are most likely genes.

Each segment in the DNA "library" must be identified as either part of a gene coding for a protein or a segment of "junk DNA." Each new gene locus that is pinpointed is a marker that makes it easier to find more new genes.

Geneticists are still not sure of the importance of the long strands of "junk DNA." But they have discovered that some of these repeating segments can be used to identify individuals. This is the basis of "DNA fingerprinting," which is now used—among

SEQUENCING A GENOME AT RECORD SPEED

Over the past twenty-five years, advances in the field of genomics have led to substantial reductions in the cost of genome sequencing. In 2003 it cost about three billion dollars and took more than a decade to complete. In 2017 the biotech firm Illumina introduced a DNA sequencing machine that could potentially decipher an entire human genome in less than an hour for a cost of less than one hundred dollars. From DNA data such as this, people can learn about sensitivity to drugs, genealogy, and information about certain genetic medical conditions.

other things—to determine family relationships and identify criminal suspects.

Next Steps for Genetics

Continuing research into the human genome—and genomes of many other organisms—will likely transform our future. Among other things, geneticists will use this information to map locations of genes causing specific disorders and develop treatments. They are tracing the history and evolution of life on Earth. They hope

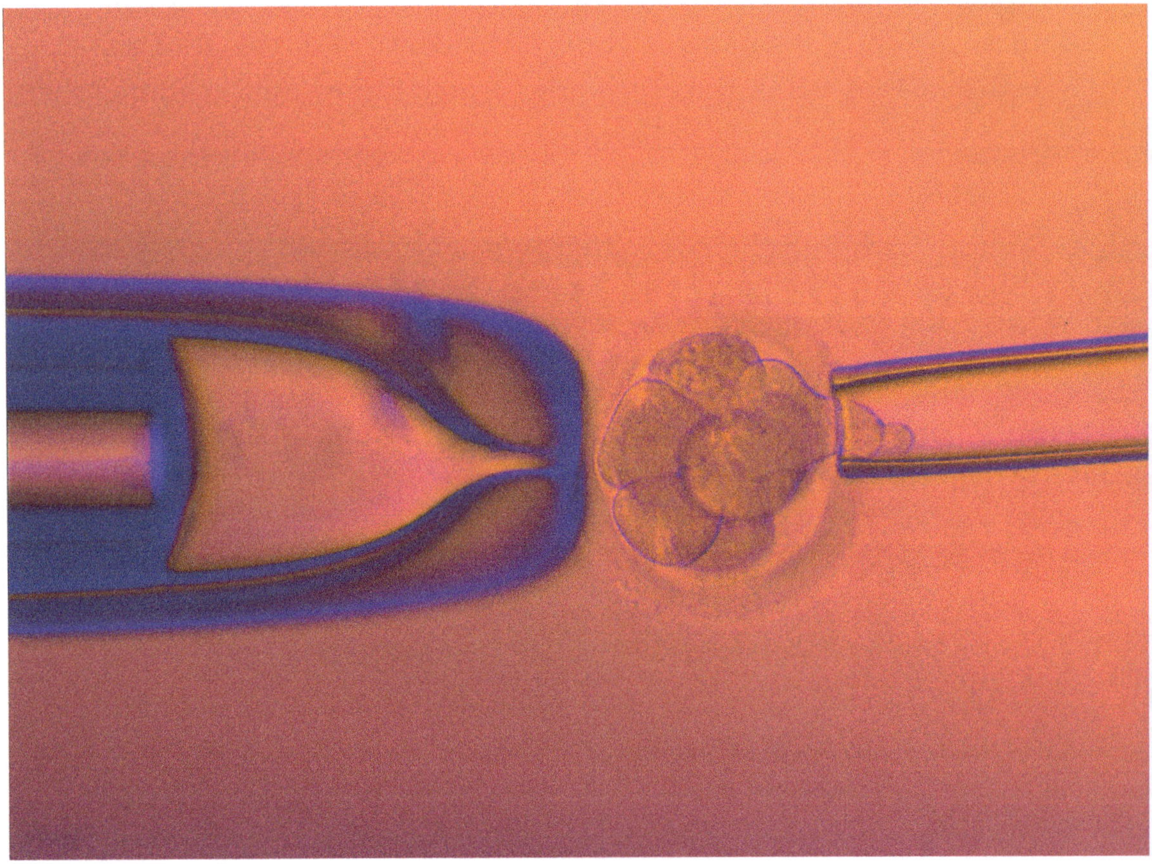

A cell from an embryo, produced by in vitro fertilization, is removed to screen for genetic disorders.

to increase understanding of how the body works, how we are related to other organisms, and how we can use genetics to benefit our culture and environment.

The science of genetic engineering continues to expand as researchers learn more about altering genes to create genetically modified plants, animals and microorganisms, and medicines. Genetic testing has helped couples having a child using in vitro fertilization (IVF). These embryos can be screened for the genetic mutations that cause cystic fibrosis, sickle cell disease, spinal muscular atrophy, and a range of other conditions. In the world of medicine, research has expanded into how gene therapy may be used to cure diseases. The world-renowned physicist Steven Hawking (1942–) said, "With genetic engineering, we will be able to increase the complexity of our DNA, and improve the human race. But it will be a slow process because one will have to wait about 18 years to see the effect of changes to the genetic code."

Bibliography

Bailey, Regina. "Genetic Variation Definition, Causes, and Examples." ThoughtCo, September 4, 2017. Retrieved October 15, 2017. https://www.thoughtco.com/genetic-variation-373457.

Briers, Demarcus. "Mendel's Law of Segregation and Assortment Simplified." DeBriers, April 19, 2012. Retrieved October 15, 2017. http://www.dbriers.com/tutorials/2012/04/mendels-law-of-segregation-assortment-simplified/.

Broad Institute of MIT and Harvard. "Human Gene Count Tumbles Again." ScienceDaily, January 15, 2008. Retrieved October 15, 2017. http://www.sciencedaily.com/releases/2008/01/080113161406.htm.

Buhr, Sandra. "Illumina Wants to Sequence Your Whole Genome for $100." TechCrunch, January 10, 2017. Retrieved October 15, 2017. https://techcrunch.com/2017/01/10/illumina-wants-to-sequence-your-whole-genome-for-100/.

"Explanation of Mendel's Three Laws Through the Discussion of Meiosis." *Seattle PI*. Retrieved October 15, 2017. http://education.seattlepi.com/explanation-mendels-three-laws-through-discussion-meiosis-3838.html.

"Genetic Engineering." Explaining the Future.com. Retrieved October 15, 2017. http://www.explainingthefuture.com/genetics.html.

"Genetic Linkage." Genetic Science Learning Center. Retrieved October 15, 2017. http://learn.genetics.utah.edu/content/pigeons/geneticlinkage.

"Genetics." *Genetics Encyclopedia.* Farmington Hills, MI: The Gale Group, Inc., 2003.

Gibbon, Ann. "The World's First Farmers Were Surprisingly Diverse." *Science*, July 14, 2016. Retrieved October 15, 2017. http://www.sciencemag.org/news/2016/07/worlds-first-farmers-were-surprisingly-diverse.

Greenwood, Tracey, and Richard Allen. *Senior Biology 1: Student Resource and Activity Manual.* Hamilton, New Zealand: Biozone International Ltd., 2004.

Hales, Karen G. "Timeline of the History of Genetics," Department of Biology, Davidson College, Davidson, NC, 2007. Retrieved October 15, 2017. http://www.bio.davidson.edu/people/kahales/301Genetics/timeline.html#top.

Lewis, Ricki. *Human Genetics: Concepts and Applications*, 8th Ed. New York, NY: McGraw Hill Higher Education, 2008.

Lobo, Ingrid. "Environmental Influences on Gene Expression." Scitable by Nature Education, 2008. Retrieved October 15, 2017. https://www.nature.com/scitable/topicpage/environmental-influences-on-gene-expression-536.

Miko, Ilona. "Gregor Mendel and the Principles of Inheritance." Scitable by Nature Education, 2008. Retrieved October 15, 2017. https://www.nature.com/scitable/topicpage/gregor-mendel-and-the-principles-of-inheritance-593.

O'Connor, Clare, and Ilona Miko. "Gene Inheritance and Transmission." 2008. Retrieved October 15, 2017. Adapted from "Developing the Chromosome Theory," *Nature Education* 1(1) and http://www.nature.com/scitable/topicpage/Developing-the-Chromosome-Theory-164.

O'Neil, Dennis. "Mendel's Genetics." 1997–2009. Retrieved October 15, 2017. http://anthro.palomar.edu/mendel/mendel_1.htm.

Pierce, Benjamin. *Genetics Solutions and Problem Solving MegaManual*, Second Edition. New York, NY: W. H. Freeman/Macmillan Learning, 2004.

Ruder, Kate, and Edward R. Winstead. "A Quick Guide to Sequenced Genomes." Genome News Network, J. Craig Venter Institute, 2004. Retrieved October 15, 2017. http://www.genomenewsnetwork.org/resources/sequenced_genomes/genome_guide_p1.shtml.

Ruse, Michael. "The Mendel-Darwin Connection." The Chronicle of Higher Education, June 1, 2010. Retrieved October 15, 2017. http://www.chronicle.com/blogs/brainstorm/the-mendel-darwin-connection/24433.

Starr, Cecie, and Ralph Taggart. *Cell Biology and Genetics*. Florence, KY: Thomson Brooks/Cole, 2006.

Timmer, John. "How Mendel Started Genetics by Getting It Mostly Wrong." ArsTechnica, April 26, 2010. Retrieved October 15, 2017. https://arstechnica.com/science/2010/04/breaking-mendels-laws-the-value-of-informative-errors/.

"What Is Cancer?" National Cancer Institute. Retrieved October 15, 2017. https://www.cancer.gov/about-cancer/understanding/what-is-cancer.

Willett, Edward. *Genetics Demystified*. New York, NY: McGraw Hill Professional, 2005.

Glossary

allele Any of several forms of a gene, usually arising through mutation, that are responsible for hereditary variation.

chromosome A structure in the cell nucleus composed of a single DNA molecule and containing many genes along its length.

dihybrid cross A genetic cross in which two traits (genes) are followed and the phenotypes counted.

diploid Having two sets of chromosomes, one set from each parent; occurs in all body cells. The diploid number of human chromosomes ($2n$) is forty-six, or twenty-three pairs.

dominant The condition in which one allele masks the presence of another (recessive) allele of the same gene.

gamete The sex cell (egg, or ovum, in females and sperm in males); each gamete has only one member of each pair of chromosomes and therefore only half the organism's genetic information.

gene The unit or factor that determines a trait; located in a DNA molecule (chromosome) inside every cell nucleus; for example, the gene for eye color.

genome The complete set of all genes in all chromosomes of an organism.

genotype The pair of alleles that combine in an organism to produce a phenotype; for example, *BB* or *Bb* for brown eye color and *bb* for blue eye color.

haploid Having one set of chromosomes; occurs in gametes as a result of meiosis (reduction division). The haploid number of human chromosomes (*n*) is twenty-three.

heterozygous Having two different alleles in the genotype; for example, *Yy*.

homologous chromosome A member of a pair of chromosomes in a diploid organism; homologous chromosome pairs are identical in size, shape, and sequence of genes.

homozygous Having two identical alleles in the genotype; for example, *YY* or *yy*.

hybrid An offspring produced by crossing two genetically different parents of different types; combines traits of both parents.

meiosis The nuclear division process used to form gametes; includes a reduction division, which halves the chromosome number and increases variation in offspring.

mitochondria Organelles in the cytoplasm of cells that functions in energy production.

mitosis The nuclear division process used in growth, maintenance, and repair of organisms; results in production of two identical daughter cells from a single parent cell.

monohybrid cross A genetic cross in which only one trait (gene) is followed and the phenotypes counted.

mutation An alteration in the genetic makeup (DNA sequence) of an organism, which affects the genotype and often the phenotype.

natural selection The primary process by which evolution occurs; results when certain genetic types in a population are more successful than others in contributing offspring to the next generation.

organelle A cell organ; a specialized part of a cell having some specific function.

phenotype The visible traits of an organism, such as eye color, seed color, or seed type.

probability The likelihood that a given event will occur; can be expressed as a fraction, decimal, or percentage (for example, ¼, 0.25, or 25%).

Punnett square A diagram illustrating the results of a cross by showing all possible combinations of genotypes.

recessive The condition in which the expression of one allele is masked by the presence of another (dominant) allele of the same gene.

selective breeding Artificially influencing the inheritance of traits by selecting the parents of each new generation.

testcross A cross between an individual displaying the dominant phenotype and a homozygous recessive individual; used to determine an individual's genotype.

Further Reading

Books

Bardoe, Cheryl. *Gregor Mendel: The Friar Who Grew Peas.* New York, NY: Abrams Books, 2015.

Braux, Alain. *GMO 101*. Austin, TX: Alain Braux International Publishing, 2014.

Croce, Nicholas. *The Science and Technology Behind the Human Genome Project.* New York, NY: Rosen/Britannica Educational Publishing, 2015.

Jackson, Tom. *Genetics: Why We Are Who We Are.* New York, NY: Cavendish Square Publishing, 2017.

Mitchell, Megan. *The Human Genome.* New York, NY: Cavendish Square Publishing, 2016.

Mukherjee, Siddhartha. *The Gene*. New York, NY: Scribner, 2016.

Rauf, Don. *DNA, RNA, and the Inheritance of Traits.* New York, NY: Enslow Publishing, 2019.

Websites

American Society of Human Genetics

www.ashg.org

This organization hosts conferences, advocates for support for genetic research, promotes genetic services, and educates the public about genetics.

Genome Canada

genomecanada.ca/en

Genome Canada is a nonprofit organization dedicated to advancing genome research for the benefit of all Canadians. The website includes a section titled "Information for the Public" that gives basic information relating genomics to agriculture, environment, forestry, and fisheries, as well as human health.

National Human Genome Research Institute

www.genome.gov

The NHGRI led the project to sequence the human genome and is now leading the research to understand its structure, function, and role in health and disease. The site has an Educational Resources section with information on the Human Genome Project plus basic genetics information.

Index